NORTH CAROLINA
TRIVIA

REVISED EDITION

NORTH CAROLINA TRIVIA

COMPILED BY
ERNIE & JILL COUCH

REVISED EDITION

Rutledge Hill Press
Nashville, Tennessee

04.95

Published by Rutledge Hill Press, 211 Seventh Avenue North,
Nashville, Tennessee 37219

Typography by Bailey Typography, Nashville, Tennessee

Library of Congress Cataloging-in-Publication Data
Couch, Ernie, 1949–
    North Carolina trivia / compiled by Ernie & Jill Couch. — Rev.
ed.
    191 p.   cm.
    ISBN 1-55853-112-2
    1. North Carolina — Miscellanea.   2. Questions and answers.
I. Couch, Jill, 1948–   .   II. Title.
F254.5.C64   1991   91-2463
975 — dc20   CIP

Printed in the United States of America
4 5 6 — 96 95

PREFACE

When *North Carolina Trivia* was originally compiled, it became evident that many volumes could be written about this fascinating state. North Carolina has a colorful and compelling history based on a richly diversified land and people. Now the revised edition of *North Carolina Trivia* captures even more interesting facts about this exciting heritage.

North Carolina Trivia is designed to be informative, educational, and entertaining. Most of all we hope that you will be motivated to learn even more about the great state of North Carolina.

Ernie & Jill Couch

To
Laveta & Clyde H. Seiler
and the
great people of North Carolina

TABLE OF CONTENTS

GEOGRAPHY 9

ENTERTAINMENT 45

HISTORY 69

ARTS & LITERATURE 105

SPORTS & LEISURE 129

SCIENCE & NATURE 163

GEOGRAPHY

Q. What is the highest point of elevation in North Carolina?

A. Mount Mitchell in Yancey County, 6,684 feet (2,037 meters) above sea level.

———◆———

Q. How many counties does North Carolina have?

A. 100.

———◆———

Q. What is the largest sound on the East Coast?

A. Pamlico Sound.

———◆———

Q. Where did 950 Indians lose their lives during a major battle northwest of Snow Hill during the Tuscarora War?

A. Nooherooka.

———◆———

Q. What is the meaning of *Carolina?*

A. "Land of Charles."

Q. What scenic highway begins in the Great Smoky Mountains of North Carolina?

A. The Blue Ridge Parkway.

Q. What coastal area is known as the "graveyard of the Atlantic"?

A. Cape Hatteras.

Q. Prior to the War Between the States, what North Carolina city had a United States mint?

A. Charlotte.

Q. Enfield, Edgecombe County's first seat, was originally called by what name?

A. Huckleberry Swamp.

Q. How many federal Indian reservations are located in North Carolina?

A. One, Cherokee Indian Reservation.

Q. What North Carolina city has the nation's first public boarding school for high school students gifted in math and science?

A. Durham, the North Carolina School of Science and Mathematics.

Q. What coastal town of approximately 200 claims to be the "seafood capital of the world"?

A. Calabash.

Q. In what community did fifty-one ladies meet on October 25, 1774, and pledge to boycott tea and other British goods?

A. Edenton.

———◆———

Q. Morrow Mountain State Park is in which county?

A. Stanly.

———◆———

Q. The largest display of old work boats in the Southeast can be seen in what North Carolina city?

A. Wilmington.

———◆———

Q. Historic Bethabara, the first Moravian settlement in North Carolina, is the site of what present-day city?

A. Winston-Salem.

———◆———

Q. Who established Kinston, originally Kingston, in 1740?

A. William Heritage.

———◆———

Q. What is the largest recreation area on the Blue Ridge Parkway?

A. Doughton Park.

———◆———

Q. In which south central county is the community of Eggtown?

A. Anson.

Q. What was the name of the site, off North Carolina's Outer Banks, where the Wright brothers flew their first powered craft?

A. Kill Devil Hills.

Q. How many square miles does the Great Dismal Swamp cover?

A. 750 square miles (1,940 square kilometers).

Q. In what historic village is the local liquor store called "Ye Olde ABC Package Store"?

A. Bath.

Q. The biggest and deadliest battle fought in North Carolina during the War Between the States took place in what county?

A. Johnson, Bentonville Battlefield.

Q. Which county seat in North Carolina has the smallest population?

A. Camden.

Q. Legend tells that Blackbeard built what house, still standing in Beaufort, as a resting place for his crew?

A. Hammock House.

Q. Kinston is the location of what Confederate gunboat sunk in 1865 and recovered in 1961?

A. The C.S.S. *Neuse*.

Q. The hill upon which the state's psychiatric facilities in Raleigh are situated is named in whose honor?

A. Dorothea L. Dix.

———◆———

Q. The North Carolina state fair is held in which city?

A. Raleigh.

———◆———

Q. Which two North Carolina governors were born near Windsor?

A. David Stone (1808–1810) and Locke Craig (1913–1917).

———◆———

Q. Where was North Carolina's first newspaper established?

A. New Bern.

———◆———

Q. The Venus's-flytrap grows naturally only within a seventy-five mile radius of what town?

A. Hampstead.

———◆———

Q. What Wilkes County community bears the name of an article of footwear?

A. Shoe.

———◆———

Q. Hertford lies on the banks of what river?

A. The Perquimans River.

Q. What city serves as the capital of North Carolina?

A. Raleigh.

Q. By what name was Connelly Springs first called?

A. Excelsior.

Q. Morganton was the home of what former United States senator who gained fame during the Watergate trial?

A. Sam Ervin.

Q. To gain recognition, which community started an annual event featuring lizard races?

A. Lizard Lick.

Q. What group of American Indians living in Robeson County is the only tribe to hold on to its native land without being forced to a reservation?

A. The Lumbee Indians.

Q. For what noted mineralogist are the rare gem hiddenite and a community in Alexander County named?

A. William Earl Hidden.

Q. What town is the site of the world's largest Marine Corps Air Station, Cherry Point?

A. Havelock.

Q. How large is North Carolina in square miles?

A. 52,586 square miles, including inland waters.

———◆———

Q. What is the only highway that runs through Pamlico County?

A. The Intracoastal Highway.

———◆———

Q. The community of Toast is found in what county?

A. Surry.

———◆———

Q. Where was Andy Griffith born?

A. Mount Airy.

———◆———

Q. What is the oldest town in Onslow County?

A. Swansboro.

———◆———

Q. Skewarky was the name first used by which Martin County town?

A. Williamston.

———◆———

Q. How many barrier islands make up the ocean front property of Brunswick County?

A. Six.

Q. Billy Graham was born and raised near what city?

A. Charlotte.

———◆———

Q. What community on the Pasquotank River received its name from building small commercial sailing vessels?

A. Shipyard.

———◆———

Q. During the 1800s, what Transylvania County town was noted for its flourishing high hat industry?

A. Brevard.

———◆———

Q. In what county can the original Tom Haywood's Kicking Machine be seen?

A. Craven.

———◆———

Q. How many inhabitants were incorporated in Rocky Mount in 1867?

A. 300.

———◆———

Q. What city serves as the agricultural wholesale center for North Carolina?

A. Asheville.

———◆———

Q. Campbell University is located in what county?

A. Harnett.

Q. What Granville County community is named for the traditional call of fox hunters when quarry is sighted?

A. Tally Ho.

———◆———

Q. The Uwharrie National Forest is in which three counties?

A. Randolph, Montgomery, and Davidson.

———◆———

Q. What is the third largest city in North Carolina?

A. Winston-Salem.

———◆———

Q. What town was selected to be the site of the first capital of the independent state of North Carolina?

A. New Bern.

———◆———

Q. What was the hometown of the world's largest twins, Billy and Benny McCrary, who each exceeded 800 pounds in weight?

A. Hendersonville.

———◆———

Q. What mansion home of railroad magnate John Aaron Wilkinson was converted to a restaurant in 1947?

A. River Forest Manor.

———◆———

Q. Texas Gulf runs a large phosphate mine five miles north of what community?

A. Aurora.

Q. A tour of what Kannapolis plant reveals the latest in weaving techniques?

A. Cannon Mills.

Q. What is the greatest distance between the eastern and western borders of North Carolina?

A. 503 miles.

Q. What structure, standing at Diamond Shoal, is America's tallest brick lighthouse?

A. The Cape Hatteras Lighthouse (208 feet tall).

Q. What county uses the slogan "Heart of the Blue Ridge"?

A. Yancey.

Q. What monument stands in the center of Thomasville, honoring its furniture industry?

A. The world's largest Duncan Phyfe chair.

Q. By 1950, what North Carolina county led the nation in the number of textile mills?

A. Gaston.

Q. The community of Oriental received its name from what incident?

A. The sinking of the *Oriental*, a Union transport, in 1862.

Q. What is the county seat of Edgecombe County?

A. Tarboro.

———◆———

Q. What restaurant is housed in the only nineteenth-century building still standing in downtown Durham?

A. Sudi's.

———◆———

Q. By what two names was South Mills formerly known?

A. New Lebanon and Gretna Green.

———◆———

Q. Near what city is the North Carolina Zoological Park?

A. Asheboro.

———◆———

Q. What does the seated figure on the state seal represent?

A. Plenty.

———◆———

Q. The Biltmore mansion, known to be the largest private house in the world, has how many rooms?

A. 250.

———◆———

Q. Hanging Rock State Park is in what county?

A. Stokes.

Q. Near what community was the farm of Lindsey Carson, father of Kit Carson?

A. Harmony.

———◆———

Q. What is the oldest brick house in North Carolina?

A. Newbold–White House, Hertford.

———◆———

Q. What is the lowest point of elevation in North Carolina?

A. Sea level, along the Atlantic Coast.

———◆———

Q. Duke University is in what city?

A. Durham.

———◆———

Q. How many representatives does the North Carolina state legislature have?

A. 120.

———◆———

Q. The Old Stone House, built in 1764, is in what county?

A. Rowan.

———◆———

Q. What was the last county created in North Carolina?

A. Avery, 1911.

Q. What town served as the terminus for the Great Dismal Swamp Canal?

A. Elizabeth City.

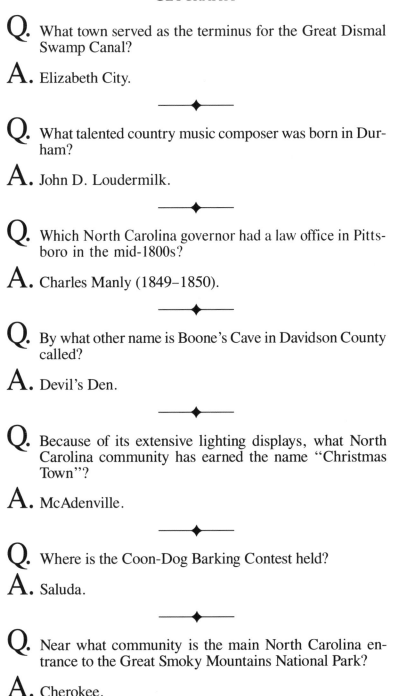

Q. What talented country music composer was born in Durham?

A. John D. Loudermilk.

Q. Which North Carolina governor had a law office in Pittsboro in the mid-1800s?

A. Charles Manly (1849–1850).

Q. By what other name is Boone's Cave in Davidson County called?

A. Devil's Den.

Q. Because of its extensive lighting displays, what North Carolina community has earned the name "Christmas Town"?

A. McAdenville.

Q. Where is the Coon-Dog Barking Contest held?

A. Saluda.

Q. Near what community is the main North Carolina entrance to the Great Smoky Mountains National Park?

A. Cherokee.

Q. What is the most common nickname given to North Carolina?

A. The Tar Heel State.

———◆———

Q. For which Revolutionary War hero was Wayne County named?

A. "Mad Anthony" Wayne.

———◆———

Q. In what scenic area is the nation's highest swinging bridge?

A. Grandfather Mountain, one mile high.

———◆———

Q. In which cemetery rest the graves of War of 1812 naval hero Otway Burns, a girl buried in a keg of rum, and Captain Josiah Pender, War Between the States commander of Fort Macon?

A. The Old Burying Ground, Beaufort.

———◆———

Q. Andy Griffith makes his summer home near what North Carolina community?

A. Manteo.

———◆———

Q. What is the length of the longest straight stretch of railroad track in the nation, which runs between Hamlet and Wilmington on the Seaboard Line?

A. 78.8 miles.

———◆———

Q. In which present-day town was Fort Dobbs situated?

A. Statesville.

Q. What is the greatest distance between the northern and southern borders of North Carolina?

A. 187 miles.

———◆———

Q. What community is home of the world's largest producer of household textiles such as sheets and towels?

A. Kannapolis.

———◆———

Q. Asheville was once known by what nickname?

A. "The City of Temples."

———◆———

Q. Where is the oldest fishing pier on the East Coast?

A. Kure Beach, New Hanover County.

———◆———

Q. What county was the site of the nation's first gold rush?

A. Cabarrus County.

———◆———

Q. What town was founded in 1710 by a few Swiss and English settlers and several hundred German Palatines?

A. New Bern.

———◆———

Q. Woodrow Wilson and, later, Dean Rusk were students at which Mecklenburg County college?

A. Davidson College.

Q. What are North Carolina's only public caverns?

A. Linville Caverns.

———◆———

Q. In 1728 an official survey established a hitherto disputed boundary between North Carolina and what neighboring colony?

A. Virginia.

———◆———

Q. 2828 Duke Homestead Road, Durham, is the address of what museum?

A. The Tobacco Museum.

———◆———

Q. What community is known as America's smallest town, with the 1980 census showing a population of eight people?

A. Dellview, Gaston County.

———◆———

Q. For whom was Battleboro named?

A. James and Joseph Battle.

———◆———

Q. Where is the Southern Baptist Convention conference center situated?

A. Ridgecrest.

———◆———

Q. What is the oldest known house in Nash County?

A. The Cooper House.

Q. At the time of his death, poet Carl Sandburg lived in what North Carolina community?

A. Flat Rock, Henderson County.

———◆———

Q. The University of North Carolina at Charlotte is surrounded by a twenty-square-mile development known by what name?

A. University City.

———◆———

Q. What forty-mile river winds through Durham, emptying into the Neuse?

A. Eno River.

———◆———

Q. By what name is U.S. Highway 158 between Elizabeth City and Fort Raleigh known?

A. The Virginia Dare Trail.

———◆———

Q. For whom was Asheboro named?

A. North Carolina Governor Samuel Ashe (1795–1798).

———◆———

Q. For whom was the community of Ennice in Alleghany County named?

A. Ennice Higgens, daughter of the first postmaster.

———◆———

Q. What crossroads received its name from a nickname given it by colonial housewives concerned about the grog houses and loose women of the area?

A. The Trap, today called Old Trap.

Q. What is the North Carolina state motto?

A. *Esse quam videri* ("To be, rather than to seem").

———◆———

Q. The grave of the first Siamese twins to gain worldwide notoriety is in which town?

A. Mount Airy, Surry County.

———◆———

Q. Where is the Haliwa-Saponi Pow Wow held each year?

A. Hollister, Halifax County.

———◆———

Q. What religious group settled Belvidere in the early eighteenth century?

A. The Quakers.

———◆———

Q. Wake Forest College, established in the community of Wake Forest in 1834, moved to what city in 1956?

A. Winston-Salem.

———◆———

Q. Nationally, where does North Carolina rank in labor unionization?

A. Fiftieth.

———◆———

Q. A 1920 book by Dr. J. C. Coggins, *Abraham Lincoln, A North Carolinian With Proof,* suggests the actual birthplace of the former president was in what county?

A. Rutherford.

Q. What city is the second oldest in the state?

A. New Bern.

———◆———

Q. The town of Atlantic was originally known by what name?

A. Hunting Quarters.

———◆———

Q. Where does North Carolina rank in population compared to the other states?

A. Tenth.

———◆———

Q. What is the name given to the shallow, oval-shaped craters in Bladen County, probably created by a meteor shower during the Pleistocene age?

A. Carolina Bays.

———◆———

Q. What town is known as the "Rockfish Capital"?

A. Weldon.

———◆———

Q. Construction of what dam made it the tallest in the eastern United States?

A. Fontana Dam, 480 feet.

———◆———

Q. Tracy Barnes, the first person to float across America in a hot air balloon (1958), selected what North Carolina county for his manufacturing plant, The Balloon Works?

A. Iredell.

Q. What nationally known news commentator was born in Wilmington?

A. David Brinkley.

———◆———

Q. Roan Mountain is in what national forest?

A. Pisgah National Forest.

———◆———

Q. How did High Point get its name?

A. It was founded on the highest point of land along the railroad between Goldsboro and Charlotte.

———◆———

Q. How many electoral votes are allocated to North Carolina?

A. Thirteen.

———◆———

Q. What community college is the largest in North Carolina?

A. Central Piedmont Community College.

———◆———

Q. The Cullasaja Gorge runs for twenty-five miles between which two communities?

A. Highlands and Franklin.

———◆———

Q. North Carolina boasts how many miles of state-maintained highways?

A. 76,000 miles, said to be the nation's largest state-maintained highway system.

Q. Which community in Caswell County was named by those who said the land was so poor that "a rabbit had to shuffle to get his rations"?

A. Rabbit Shuffle.

Q. Where was Andrew Johnson, the seventeenth president of the United States, born?

A. Raleigh.

Q. The Croatan Indian Normal School, founded in 1887 as the nation's first four-year college for Indians, is situated on what present-day campus?

A. Pembroke State University Old Main.

Q. What community calls itself the "town that isn't a town"?

A. Butner.

Q. William E. Dodd, who served as the ambassador to Germany during the 1930s, was born in which North Carolina town?

A. Clayton.

Q. What is the largest commercial port in North Carolina?

A. Wilmington.

Q. Where did James William Cannon and his brother David build their first yarn mill in 1877?

A. Concord.

Q. What community is the largest bright-leaf-tobacco market in the Western Hemisphere?

A. Wilson.

---◆---

Q. Lord Cornwallis had the main streets in what town paved with cobblestones in 1781?

A. Hillsborough.

---◆---

Q. What is the chief mountain range in North Carolina?

A. The Blue Ridge Mountains.

---◆---

Q. Where is the oldest functioning lifesaving station in North Carolina?

A. The Oregon Inlet Coast Guard Station.

---◆---

Q. Approximately how many incorporated cities and towns are in North Carolina?

A. 465.

---◆---

Q. What present-day regional university, situated in Pasquotank County, was established in 1891 as a normal and training school for Negro students?

A. Elizabeth City State.

---◆---

Q. In what county is the Bunker Hill Covered Bridge?

A. Catawba County.

Q. What county name is taken from a Yeopin Indian word meaning "land of beautiful women"?

A. Perquimans.

———◆———

Q. Where in Warren County is the grave of Annie Carter Lee, daughter of General Robert E. Lee?

A. Jones Springs.

———◆———

Q. By what name was the Lumber (Lumbee) River first called?

A. Drowning Creek.

———◆———

Q. What states border Ashe County?

A. Tennessee and Virginia.

———◆———

Q. What historical event took place at Bennett Place, two miles west of Durham?

A. Confederate Army General Joseph E. Johnston surrendered his troops to Union General William T. Sherman.

———◆———

Q. Where in 1787 was Andrew Jackson admitted into the law profession?

A. Richmond.

———◆———

Q. What is the world's largest black-managed financial institution?

A. North Carolina Mutual Life Insurance Company, Durham.

Q. Piedmont Airlines once had a hub at what international airport?

A. Charlotte/Douglas.

Q. Which political party has dominated North Carolina's history?

A. The Democratic Party.

Q. Boogertown is situated in which county?

A. Gaston County.

Q. Wake Forest is the home of what seminary?

A. The Southeastern Baptist Theological Seminary.

Q. From an engineering standpoint, what bridge near Linville is considered the world's most complicated?

A. The Linn Cove Viaduct on the Blue Ridge Parkway.

Q. Siler City is in which county?

A. Chatham.

Q. Where are Squire and Sarah Boone, Daniel Boone's parents, buried?

A. Joppa Cemetery, a mile northwest of Mocksville, Davie County.

Q. Which town is located in both Edgecombe and Nash counties, with the railroad tracks marking the county line down the middle of Main Street?

A. Rocky Mount.

Q. The home of Governor Thomas W. Bickett (1917–1921) is in which town?

A. Louisburg.

Q. How far is Winston-Salem from the Blue Ridge Mountains?

A. About thirty miles.

Q. In what community is the famous blacksmith shop of Bea and Mike Hensley, who have created functional works for homes of famous people as well as for the Smithsonian Institution?

A. Spruce Pine.

Q. Where was the first soybean processing plant built?

A. Elizabeth City, 1912.

Q. What land region boasts the richest farmlands in North Carolina?

A. The Atlantic Coastal Plain.

Q. Department store magnate John Montgomery Belk served as mayor of which city from 1969 to 1977?

A. Charlotte.

Q. What was the name of Carl Sandburg's North Carolina farm?

A. Connemara.

Q. What nickname was given to the Fayetteville and Western plank road?

A. "The Appian Way of North Carolina."

Q. What metro area did the *Rand-McNally Places Almanac* rate first in North Carolina and twenty-third in the nation?

A. Durham.

Q. From what county was Jones County formed in 1779?

A. Craven.

Q. Where is the grave of schoolteacher Peter Stewart Ney, believed by many to be Napoleon's famous general Marshal Michael Ney, known as "Red Peter"?

A. Cleveland, Rowan County.

Q. What mountain in Pisgah National Forest has the highest cliff east of the Rocky Mountains?

A. Whiteside Mountain.

Q. Who donated the land in 1768 upon which Windsor was built?

A. John Gray.

Q. Which United States Senator was born in Monroe?

A. Jesse Helms.

———◆———

Q. What stream and community were named for the Sissipa-haw, or Saxapahaw, Indians?

A. Haw River.

———◆———

Q. On what college campus is Boiling Springs situated?

A. Gardner Webb College.

———◆———

Q. By what name was Calabash known prior to 1873?

A. Pea Landing.

———◆———

Q. What is the largest trucking company in North Carolina?

A. Carolina Freight Carriers.

———◆———

Q. Columbus County is bordered by what state?

A. South Carolina.

———◆———

Q. What creek in Rutherford County was named by worried settlers puzzled whether their horses could cross because of quicksand?

A. Puzzle Creek.

Q. Around what natural lake was part of Ocracoke built?

A. Silver Lake.

———◆———

Q. What historic area of Raleigh is known for its turn-of-the-century Victorian homes?

A. Oakwood.

———◆———

Q. What North Carolina courthouse is the oldest structure still in use?

A. The Chowan County Courthouse, 1767.

———◆———

Q. Henderson serves as the county seat of what county?

A. Vance.

———◆———

Q. What island on the Pasquotank River at Elizabeth City was named by combining the first two letters of each of the owner's four children's names?

A. Machelhe Island, for Mary, Charles, Eloise, and Helen.

———◆———

Q. The James K. Polk Memorial State Historic Site is in what community?

A. Pineville.

———◆———

Q. What is the nickname of the area surrounding Boone?

A. "The Roof of Eastern America."

Q. What North Carolina community is the world's largest producer of denim?

A. Erwin.

———◆———

Q. Bingham School, North Carolina's first military school, was established in what town in 1826?

A. Williamsboro.

———◆———

Q. What Sanford landmark, built in 1772, is called the "House in the Horseshoe"?

A. Alston House, home of Gov. Benjamin Williams.

———◆———

Q. What community received its name for being the highest point on the right-of-way of the Raleigh and Augusta Railroad between Norfolk and Sanford?

A. Apex.

———◆———

Q. What North Carolina town was named for a French industrialist?

A. Badin, for Adrien Badin.

———◆———

Q. The nation's oldest continuously working water mill, built around 1745, is still in operation today just south of what community?

A. Oak Ridge.

———◆———

Q. To which state did the Tuscarora Indians of North Carolina emigrate?

A. New York State.

Q. Mount Mitchell was known by what name before 1835 when Dr. Elisha Mitchell measured it?

A. Black Dome.

———◆———

Q. What incorporated town in North Carolina will permit horses, but not motorized vehicles, on its main street?

A. The "Western" town of Love Valley.

———◆———

Q. In 1891, what area became the first suburb of Charlotte?

A. Dilworth.

———◆———

Q. *The Lookout,* built in 1862 and now the oldest known working tugboat in existence, is berthed at what marina when not in use?

A. Salty Dog Marina, Manteo.

———◆———

Q. In whose honor was Beaufort County named?

A. Henry Somerset, Duke of Beaufort.

———◆———

Q. What community developed on the antebellum plantation of James Battle?

A. Richlands.

———◆———

Q. Who established a pre-Civil War buggy factory in Kinston?

A. The Dibble family.

Q. For whom was Rockingham named in 1784?

A. Charles Watson Wentworth, Marquis of Rockingham.

———◆———

Q. Where was the first tobacco sales warehouse built in 1866 solely to age cured leaf tobacco?

A. Oxford.

———◆———

Q. The Alamance Battlefield is situated near which town?

A. Burlington.

———◆———

Q. In what community is the Museum of North Carolina Traditional Pottery?

A. Seagrove.

———◆———

Q. What community is the third oldest in North Carolina?

A. Beaufort.

———◆———

Q. By what nickname is U.S. Highway 301 through North Carolina known?

A. "The Tobacco Trail."

———◆———

Q. The second-smallest post office in the United States may be seen in what North Carolina community?

A. Salvo, Dare County (8 feet × 12 feet).

Q. Ocracoke lies within the boundary of what county?

A. Hyde.

———◆———

Q. What town was originally named Magnetic City?

A. Buladean.

———◆———

Q. Where does North Carolina rank in area among all the states?

A. Twenty-eighth.

———◆———

Q. Joshua Barnes is known as "the father" of which county?

A. Wilson.

———◆———

Q. In 1910 Heriot Clarkson founded what community as a summer colony?

A. Little Switzerland.

———◆———

Q. What land region in North Carolina has the largest population?

A. The Piedmont.

———◆———

Q. What town is situated at the confluence of the Dan and Mayo rivers?

A. Mayodan.

Q. What city has the largest population in North Carolina?

A. Charlotte.

———◆———

Q. In what town did John Cobb Washington and George Washington, both relatives of President Washington, establish a shoe factory prior to the War Between the States?

A. Kinston.

———◆———

Q. Major Orren R. Smith, designer of the Confederate "Stars and Bars" flag, was a resident of what county?

A. Franklin.

———◆———

Q. By what name is the 1875 Currituck Beach Lighthouse generally known?

A. Whaleshead.

———◆———

Q. What river is said to have been named after an Indian princess who drowned herself after losing her lover?

A. Toe River, after the Indian princess Estatoe.

———◆———

Q. Shingle Landing is the former name of what Currituck County community?

A. Moyock.

———◆———

Q. What city is the site of the world's largest furniture show?

A. High Point.

Q. In what town is the tomb of Mrs. Stephen A. Douglas?

A. Reidsville.

◆

Q. What was the name of the Amish–Mennonite community that existed in the northeast corner of North Carolina from 1907 to 1935?

A. Pudding Ridge.

◆

Q. What part of Currituck County may only be entered by road from Virginia?

A. The Knotts Island area.

◆

Q. In 1783, what Methodist circuit-riding preacher named a North Carolina community after his hometown of Sligo in Ireland?

A. The Reverend Edward Drumgoole.

◆

Q. What town has been called "the pickle capital of the South"?

A. Mount Olive.

◆

Q. By what name was Robbins originally called?

A. Mechanicsville.

◆

Q. Which county contains the geographical center of North Carolina?

A. Chatham, ten miles northwest of Sanford.

Q. Which county is the least populated?

A. Tyrrell.

———◆———

Q. The famous Confederate naval Captain, James Iredell Waddell, was born in what town in 1824?

A. Pittsboro.

———◆———

Q. What is the only county in the United States to have a complete range of mountains within the county?

A. Stokes (Sauratown Range).

———◆———

Q. Which states border North Carolina?

A. Virginia, Tennessee, Georgia, and South Carolina.

———◆———

Q. In what Moore County town did Andrew Johnson work as a tailor?

A. Carthage.

———◆———

Q. What town developed around Brock Mill Pond?

A. Trenton.

———◆———

Q. In what community is the 1808-built Sally-Billy House part of the historical district?

A. Halifax.

Q. Onion Falls is on what river in Jackson County?

A. West Fork Tuckasegee River.

◆

Q. In what county is Surf City situated?

A. Pender.

◆

Q. What creek and community in the western part of Mitchell County were named for the now-extinct passenger pigeon?

A. Pigeonroost.

◆

Q. What coastal county was formed in 1870 from Currituck, Hyde, and Tyrrell counties?

A. Dare County.

◆

Q. The Quick community in Caswell County was originally known by what name?

A. Kill Quick.

◆

Q. What Jackson County town was named for an early Danish newspaperman of the area?

A. Sylva, for William Sylva.

ENTERTAINMENT

C H A P T E R   T W O

Q. What North Carolina actress starred in the hit television series "Topper"?

A. Anne Jeffreys.

◆

Q. In 1977, what three organizations worked to bring theatrical productions to North Carolina public television?

A. Carolina Regional Theatre, UNC–TV, and the Department of Radio, Television and Motion Pictures of the University of North Carolina.

◆

Q. What movie, written and directed by Stephen King and filmed in Wilmington, features a convoy of eighteen-wheelers running rampant?

A. *Maximum Overdrive.*

◆

Q. What water theme park is located just south of Greensboro?

A. Water Country USA.

◆

Q. Where was country music star Ronnie Milsap born?

A. Robinsville.

Q. What male actor starred in the North Carolina film, *Last American Hero,* based on the early life of race car driver Junior Johnson?

A. Jeff Bridges.

———◆———

Q. Where is the Cabarrus County Fair held each September?

A. Concord.

———◆———

Q. What noted singer, pianist, and arranger was born in Tryon?

A. Nina Simone.

———◆———

Q. *Listen and Remember,* an outdoor drama telling the story of early pioneers, including the parents of Andrew Jackson, is presented in what community?

A. Waxhaw.

———◆———

Q. What was Andy Griffith's first million-selling comedy album, recorded at Greensboro?

A. *What It Was Was Football.*

———◆———

Q. During the annual Square-Up Celebration at Union Grove, what unusual dance style is exhibited?

A. The Smooth Big Circle Appalachian Style Dance.

———◆———

Q. Gospel singer Shirley Ceasar began her career as a member of what Durham singing group?

A. The Charity Singers.

Q. What motion picture executive was born in Wilson and served as casting director and story editor for Otto Preminger from 1962 to 1969?

A. Bill Barnes.

———◆———

Q. In what community was singer Donna Fargo born?

A. Mount Airy.

———◆———

Q. *Blackbeard's Revenge,* an outdoor drama depicting Blackbeard's life before becoming the infamous pirate, is performed in what community?

A. Swansboro.

———◆———

Q. Grace Kelly starred in what 1950s motion picture filmed at the Biltmore Mansion?

A. *The Swan.*

———◆———

Q. What "high-flying" festival is held at West Onslow Beach?

A. The Kite Festival.

———◆———

Q. What award-winning recording artist was born in Black Mountain?

A. Roberta Flack.

———◆———

Q. Carroll O'Connor, better known to television audiences as Archie Bunker, attended what North Carolina school?

A. Wake Forest College.

Q. What name is given to the children's pageant at the Tyrrell County Potato Festival?

A. The Tator Tot Contest.

———◆———

Q. What North Carolina-born professional basketball player appeared in the movie *The Fish that Saved Pittsburgh?*

A. Meadowlark Lemon.

———◆———

Q. The television movies *A Stoning in Fulham County* and *The Ryan White Story* were shot in what town?

A. Statesville.

———◆———

Q. Fiddler Charlie Daniels was born in what North Carolina city?

A. Wilmington.

———◆———

Q. The story of Tom Dula is depicted each summer in what outdoor drama presented in Wilkes County?

A. *The Legend of Tom Dooley.*

———◆———

Q. In which town is the Oak Hollow Fiddlers Festival held?

A. High Point.

———◆———

Q. Wadesboro was the birthplace of what noted guitarist?

A. Blind Boy Fuller.

Q. The adventures of Blackbeard the pirate are brought to life each summer in what outdoor drama?

A. *Blackbeard: Knight of the Black Flag.*

———◆———

Q. What movie studios boast the largest cyclorama stage in the world?

A. Hollywood East, E. O. Studios, Shelby.

———◆———

Q. What Lenoir native won an Emmy in 1978 for his portrayal of Matt Powers on "The Doctors"?

A. James Pritchett.

———◆———

Q. Actor and educator Earle Hyman was born in which North Carolina town?

A. Rocky Mount.

———◆———

Q. What 1982 film made in North Carolina portrays a drunken British poet upsetting a New England community?

A. *Reuben, Reuben.*

———◆———

Q. In what summer event at Sparta are the contestants machines?

A. The annual Sparta Tractor Pull.

———◆———

Q. Kerr Lake is the site of what annual gospel music event?

A. The Annual Gospel Singing on the Lake.

Q. In what movie did Andy Griffith have his first big role?

A. *No Time for Sergeants.*

———◆———

Q. What Black Mountain establishment is devoted to dulcimers, psaltries, and unusual string instruments?

A. Song of the Wood.

———◆———

Q. During the summer months, what outdoor drama relives the story of the Cherokee Indians?

A. *Unto These Hills.*

———◆———

Q. Joseph Leonard ("Joe") Bonner, pianist and composer, was born in what Coastal Plain city?

A. Rocky Mount.

———◆———

Q. Good times, food, and fellowship are the order of the day on Dare Day in what community?

A. Manteo.

———◆———

Q. Jesse Helms served in what capacity at Raleigh radio station WRAL, 1948–1951?

A. News and program director.

———◆———

Q. Ronnie Milsap won what coveted award from the Country Music Association in 1977?

A. Entertainer of the Year.

Q. Laurinburg-born Woody Shaw acquired fame playing what instrument?

A. Trumpet.

Q. Which blues harmonica player from Kings Mountain was taught to play by his uncle, Sonny Terry?

A. J. C. Burris.

Q. Nina Simone's version of what song yielded her a hit record in 1959?

A. "I Loves You Porgy."

Q. For what television special series did Charles Kuralt, a Wilmington native, win an Emmy in 1969?

A. *On the Road with Charles Kuralt*.

Q. Kermit Hunter's *The Rising Splendor* is a drama about what historic place?

A. Tryon Palace.

Q. Singer Del Reeves was born in what North Carolina community?

A. Sparta.

Q. What was the name of banjo picker Charlie Poole's bluegrass band of the 1920s and 1930s?

A. The North Carolina Ramblers.

Q. What action-packed gangster melodrama was filmed in North Carolina in 1950?

A. *Highway 301.*

Q. Spivey's Corner gained national recognition for what contest whose participants have appeared on Johnny Carson's "The Tonight Show"?

A. National Hollerin' Contest.

Q. What festival is held in Mount Airy each October?

A. The Autumn Leaves Festival.

Q. Actress Frances Bavier retired to what North Carolina community?

A. Siler City.

Q. What outdoor drama tells the story of Henry Berry Lowrie and the Lumbee Indians?

A. *Strike at the Wind*, Pembroke.

Q. What band leader, saxophonist, and composer born in Hamlet had a great influence on the history of jazz?

A. John William Coltrane.

Q. What famous comedian was born in Franklinton, near Wake Forest?

A. Soupy Sales.

Q. What famous southern gospel music group is headquartered in Asheville?

A. The Kingsmen.

———◆———

Q. What Michael Cimino film was partially shot in North Carolina?

A. *Year of the Dragon.*

———◆———

Q. The Bright Leaf Hoedown is a fall event in what town?

A. Yanceyville.

———◆———

Q. What North Carolina-born actress has appeared on stage and in several motion pictures, including *Kiss Me Kate* and *Show Boat?*

A. Kathryn Grayson.

———◆———

Q. Born and raised near Wilson, blues musician Alden ("Allen") Bunn was noted for what instrument?

A. Guitar.

———◆———

Q. What community is known for its New Year's Shooters festivities in which the firing of black powder muskets ushers in the new year?

A. Cherryville.

———◆———

Q. Entertainer Earl Scruggs was born in what county?

A. Cleveland.

Q. What is the name of America's oldest symphonic outdoor drama?

A. *The Lost Colony,* presented on Roanoke Island since 1937.

———◆———

Q. Mooresville-born Wisner McCamey Washam became head writer in 1971 for what TV soap opera?

A. "All My Children."

———◆———

Q. What community celebrates gospel music by hosting the nation's biggest and oldest gospel singing?

A. Benson.

———◆———

Q. What is Nina Simone's actual name?

A. Eunice Waymon.

———◆———

Q. While living at Banner Elk, Marjorie Kinnan Rawlings wrote what famous novel, later turned into a movie starring Gregory Peck?

A. *The Yearling.*

———◆———

Q. What was Andy Griffith's occupation before becoming a well-known comedian and actor?

A. High school English teacher at Goldsboro.

———◆———

Q. What Sandhills area band was called by the *Washington Post* "one of the best traditional jazz bands in the country"?

A. Buck Creek Jazz Band.

Q. What North Carolina-filmed thriller starred Natalie Wood and Christopher Walken?

A. *Brainstorm.*

———◆———

Q. Chapel Hill-born blues musician, Floyd ("Dipper Boy") Council was also known by what other nickname?

A. "Devil's Daddy-In-Law."

———◆———

Q. What Elkin restaurant is housed in a restored 1896 mill?

A. Scheibers Jolly Mill Restaurant.

———◆———

Q. What group did Earl Scruggs form in 1969?

A. The Earl Scruggs Review.

———◆———

Q. Where was actress Kathryn Grayson born?

A. Winston-Salem.

———◆———

Q. Shaped note singing, pickin', and clog dancing are all a part of what Union Grove festival?

A. Old Time Fiddlers' and Bluegrass Festival.

———◆———

Q. What nationally-syndicated Christian television talk show is headquartered near Charlotte?

A. "The PTL Club."

Q. What famous bandleader of the 1940s was born in Rocky Mount?

A. Kay Kyser.

---◆---

Q. What Tar Heel-born singer/songwriter is best known for her hits "Funny Face" and "I'm the Happiest Girl in the U.S.A."?

A. Donna Fargo.

---◆---

Q. The Croaker Queen contest is held in what community?

A. Oriental.

---◆---

Q. What was the title of Roberta Flack's first album?

A. "First Take."

---◆---

Q. In what television series did Meadowlark Lemon appear during 1979?

A. "Hello Larry."

---◆---

Q. Clinton is host to what unusual beauty pageant?

A. The Eastern North Carolina Ugly Pick-up Truck Contest.

---◆---

Q. Thelma Ritter won an Academy Award nomination for what movie filmed in North Carolina?

A. *The Mating Season*.

Q. Where in North Carolina would you go to participate in the National Pumpkin Festival?

A. Spring Hope.

———◆———

Q. Bill Wooten of Statesville, an avid movie buff, has gathered the world's second largest collection of memorabilia on what great movie classic?

A. *Gone With the Wind.*

———◆———

Q. What songwriter who attended the University of North Carolina has to his credit the theme songs of such television shows as "Maude," "Alice," and "Good Times"?

A. Alan Bergman.

———◆———

Q. In what mansion are costumed "living dramas" held during tours?

A. Poplar Grove Plantation.

———◆———

Q. The North Carolina Rhododendron Festival, complete with beauty pageants and street square dancing, is held in what town?

A. Bakersville.

———◆———

Q. Wilmington and the Northeast Cape Fear Bridge are scenes for what heavy-metal horror movie?

A. *Trick or Treat.*

———◆———

Q. What resident of Raleigh was best known for her rendition of "God Bless America"?

A. Kate Smith.

Q. What North Carolina-born recording artist first came to national recognition with the hit "What A Difference You've Made In My Life"?

A. Ronnie Milsap.

◆

Q. *First for Freedom* is the historical drama presented during July and August in what community?

A. Halifax.

◆

Q. What lovable role did Frances Bavier play on the "Andy Griffith Show"?

A. Aunt Bee.

◆

Q. What country music star was born in Shelby?

A. Don Gibson.

◆

Q. What is the name of the Carowinds showplace that draws top-name performers?

A. The Paladium.

◆

Q. Bryson City serves as headquarters for what traditional southern gospel quartet?

A. The Inspirationals.

◆

Q. Where may you view the highest fireworks display in the eastern United States?

A. Beech Mountain.

Q. In what community was actress Anne Jeffreys born?

A. Goldsboro.

◆

Q. North Carolina-born George Hamilton IV recorded what 1963 hit song?

A. "Abilene."

◆

Q. What outdoor drama depicts the life of North Carolina Quakers torn between their religious beliefs and the beginnings of patriotic rebellion during the American Revolution?

A. *The Sword of Peace*, Snow Camp.

◆

Q. Where was the great motion picture director and producer Cecil B. DeMille born?

A. Washington.

◆

Q. A native of Wilmington, what bassist helped found the Modern Jazz Quartet?

A. Percy Heath.

◆

Q. What annual contest is held at Newport?

A. Pig Cookin' Contest.

◆

Q. Who starred in the movie *Thunder Road*, filmed in North Carolina in 1958?

A. Robert Mitchum.

Q. What pianist and composer wrote "Something In Blue" and "The Man I Love"?

A. Thelonius Sphere Monk.

───────◆───────

Q. What Greensboro-born rock and roll/country performer was named Most Promising Male Vocalist by *Music City News* in 1972?

A. Billy Crash Craddock.

───────◆───────

Q. A spitting contest, a greased pig contest, and horse and buggy rides are just a few of the forms of entertainment to be enjoyed at what July event in Old Fort?

A. The Old Fort Freedom Celebration.

───────◆───────

Q. What Winston-Salem–born actress appeared in *Beyond the Valley of the Dolls?*

A. Pam Grier.

───────◆───────

Q. The Annual Soldiers Reunion Celebration, the oldest patriotic event of its kind in the nation, is held in what town?

A. Newton.

───────◆───────

Q. At which North Carolina mansion was Peter Sellers's last movie filmed?

A. The Biltmore.

───────◆───────

Q. What is Soupy Sales's original name?

A. Milton Hines.

Q. What award-winning television movie was made about the life of Brian Piccolo?

A. "Brian's Song."

Q. Actor/writer Mike Evans, best known for his work on "The Jeffersons" and "Good Times," was born in what community?

A. Salisbury.

Q. The Fiddlers Convention and Buck Dance Contest is held annually in what community?

A. Newton.

Q. In what movie did country singer Margie Bowes make her first appearance?

A. *Gold Guitar.*

Q. What saxophonist from Baden is known for performing blues-based, funky music?

A. Lou Donaldson.

Q. What music festival held in Cliffside is named in honor of one of North Carolina's all-time greatest banjo pickers?

A. The Snuffy Jenkins Oldtime and Bluegrass Festival.

Q. Where are Rutherford All-County Band Concerts held?

A. Spindale.

Q. What is the title of the outdoor drama presented in Valdese, depicting the struggles of the Waldensian settlers?

A. *From This Day Forward.*

———◆———

Q. Leading man George Grizzard, who starred in *From the Terrace, Advise and Consent, Warning Shot,* and *Happy Birthday, Wanda June,* was born in what North Carolina town?

A. Roanoke Rapids.

———◆———

Q. With what record label did Roberta Flack sign in 1969?

A. Atlantic Records.

———◆———

Q. Andy Griffith portrayed what character during the five seasons he performed in the outdoor drama, *Lost Colony?*

A. Sir Walter Raleigh.

———◆———

Q. What North Carolina-born entertainer won a Grammy award for Single of the Year, "Devil Went Down to Georgia"?

A. Charlie Daniels.

———◆———

Q. Country singer George Hamilton IV was born in what city?

A. Winston-Salem.

———◆———

Q. At the age of eleven, where did John D. Loudermilk have his own top-rated country music radio program?

A. Durham.

Q. Earl Scruggs wrote the musical score for what movie?

A. *Where the Lilies Bloom.*

———◆———

Q. Who is the Roxboro-born singer and guitarist who won Pet Milk Company's 1958 nationwide talent contest?

A. Margie Bowes.

———◆———

Q. What North Carolina-made film was based on the novelette, *Cycle of the Werewolf?*

A. *The Silver Bullet.*

———◆———

Q. *Crimes of the Heart,* filmed thirty miles south of Wilmington, starred which three well-known actresses?

A. Sissy Spacek, Jessica Lange, and Diane Keaton.

———◆———

Q. Where was character actor Sidney Blackmer born?

A. Salisbury.

———◆———

Q. What guitarist, born in Nashville, North Carolina, specializes in unaccompanied, unamplified, six-string Spanish guitar?

A. Willie ("Bill") Harris.

———◆———

Q. What Southport home was used as a setting for *Firestarter?*

A. Orton Plantation.

Q. Cannon Village in Kannapolis is the host of what Spring event?

A. The Spring Fever Festival.

Q. Weston Wilbur Little, born in Parmele, became a superb soloist and accompanist on what instrument?

A. Bass.

Q. What screen writer/producer born in Charlotte in 1929 has to his credits such motion pictures as *The Greatest Story Ever Told* and *The Cheyenne Social Club?*

A. James Lee Barrett.

Q. Shot on location in North Carolina, what film starred Burt Reynolds, Loni Anderson, and Jim Nabors?

A. *Stroker Ace.*

Q. In what city was vaudeville performer and jazz singer Lena Wilson born?

A. Charlotte.

Q. Donna Fargo graduated from what North Carolina institution of higher learning?

A. High Point College.

Q. What festival is held in early October in Snow Hill?

A. The Molasses Festival.

Q. What was the last movie in which North Carolina-born actor Sidney Blackmer appeared?

A. *Rosemary's Baby.*

———◆———

Q. Kenansville hosts what drama depicting the history of Duplin County?

A. *The Liberty Cart: A Duplin Story.*

———◆———

Q. What Greenville-born pianist, composer, and educator was musical director for the David Frost television show during the years 1969–1972?

A. William ("Billy") Taylor.

———◆———

Q. What two number one hit singles did Don Gibson have in 1957?

A. "Blue, Blue Day" and "Oh, Lonesome Me."

———◆———

Q. In what city was legendary jazz musician Theolonius Monk born?

A. Rocky Mount.

———◆———

Q. What special event at Elizabeth City features activities and entertainment of the showboat era?

A. The Riverspree Festival.

———◆———

Q. What festival is held at Waynesville in August of each year?

A. The Haywood County Smoky Mountain Folk Festival.

Q. What is the second largest fair in North Carolina?

A. The Dixie Classic Fair, Winston-Salem.

———◆———

Q. Before stardom, singer Roberta Flack taught music and English literature in what community?

A. Farmville.

———◆———

Q. Country music performer Del Reeves recorded his first Top Ten hit in 1961 by what title?

A. "Be Quiet Mind."

———◆———

Q. What was the title of Peter Sellers's last movie, filmed in North Carolina?

A. *Being There.*

———◆———

Q. Kay Kyser, his band, and Ann Miller starred in what 1944 Columbia film?

A. *Carolina Blues.*

———◆———

Q. What John Wayne movie was partly filmed in North Carolina?

A. *The Green Berets.*

———◆———

Q. Noted Blues trombonist Clyde Edric Barron Bernhardt was born in 1905 in what North Carolina community?

A. Gold Hill.

Q. What Alleghany County town is known for its Halloween Parade?

A. Sparta.

———◆———

Q. What movie, filmed in North Carolina and starring Sissy Spacek, depicted corruption in the state of Tennessee?

A. *Marie.*

———◆———

Q. What Rocky Mount native played various instruments backing up Aretha Franklin in the early 1970s?

A. Harold Edward Vick.

———◆———

Q. What North Carolina film starring Richard Chamberlain and Yvette Mimieux tells the story of early happenings in the marriage of a poor teenage student?

A. *Joy in the Morning.*

———◆———

Q. Blues banjo player and guitarist Elizabeth ("Libba") Cotten was born in what town in 1892?

A. Chapel Hill.

———◆———

Q. Where is the Honeyhouse Festival held each June?

A. Belews Creek.

———◆———

Q. What was the stage name of country music performer Myrtle Wiseman, a Boone native?

A. Lulu Belle.

Q. What Raleigh-born musician, known for playing saxophone, oboe, and flute, became interested in bagpipes and started playing them professionally?

A. Rufus Harley.

———◆———

Q. Love Valley is the site of what uproarious western event?

A. The Frontier Week Rodeo.

———◆———

Q. What self-taught pianist, a native of Red Springs, has accompanied such great musicians as Dizzy Gillespie, Sarah Vaughn, Pearl Bailey, and Joe Williams?

A. John Malachi.

———◆———

Q. What 1952 motion picture starring Jennifer Jones and Charlton Heston tells the story of the stormy upbringing of a North Carolina girl?

A. *Ruby Gentry.*

———◆———

Q. What Durham-born drummer/singer was a member of "The Tonight Show" band from 1968 to 1974?

A. Grady Tate.

———◆———

Q. At what spring event in Albemarle do crafts and entertainment abound?

A. Mayfest.

———◆———

Q. What was country singer Stonewall Jackson's number one hit in 1959?

A. "Waterloo."

HISTORY

Q. Prior to 1829, what mine in North Carolina was the sole source of gold for the Philadelphia mint?

A. Reed Gold Mine.

———◆———

Q. What was North Carolina's first newspaper?

A. *North Carolina Gazette*, 1751.

———◆———

Q. A law prohibiting what activity in the hallways of the Davie County Courthouse was passed in 1866?

A. Horseback riding.

———◆———

Q. On August 18, 1587, who became the first child born of English parents in the New World?

A. Virginia Dare.

———◆———

Q. What Greensboro university is Jesse Jackson's alma mater?

A. North Carolina A & T State.

Q. What building in Edenton served as a base for Whig activities during the Revolution?

A. Chowan County Courthouse.

———◆———

Q. How many Indian tribes did John Lawson list as living in North Carolina in 1709?

A. Twenty-nine.

———◆———

Q. The Reverend Madison Lindsay, who established the Wadsworth Congregational Christian Church, Jamestown, was earlier employed by Henry Wadsworth Longfellow in what capacity?

A. Valet.

———◆———

Q. North Carolina led the world in the production of what type of products between 1720 and 1870?

A. Naval stores, pitch, rosin, tar, and turpentine.

———◆———

Q. How many free blacks lived in North Carolina at the beginning of the War Between the States?

A. 30,463 free blacks.

———◆———

Q. What college for blacks was established in Greensboro in 1891?

A. The North Carolina Agricultural and Mechanical College for the Colored Race.

———◆———

Q. Where was the first printing press put into operation in the colony of North Carolina, in June of 1749?

A. New Bern.

Q. Who in 1935 became the first female commercial pilot to solo in North Carolina?

A. Frances Dority Bray.

———◆———

Q. What was North Carolina's first state capital?

A. Bath, 1744.

———◆———

Q. Why did Blackbeard, America's most notorious pirate, come to Bath?

A. To wed his thirteenth wife.

———◆———

Q. On July 25, 1729, North Carolina gained what governmental status?

A. Royal colony.

———◆———

Q. What was the name of the county that served as the only organized government within the present boundaries of North Carolina from 1667 to 1689?

A. Albemarle.

———◆———

Q. What attraction near Greensboro includes a research center and computer facilities devoted to North Carolina black history?

A. Charlotte Hawkins Brown Memorial.

———◆———

Q. Numerically, where does James K. Polk rank among the nation's presidents?

A. Eleventh.

Q. The first American battleship commissioned for World War II, the U.S.S. *North Carolina,* was given what nickname?

A. "Showboat."

Q. In what year did North Carolina pass its first cigarette tax?

A. 1969.

Q. The Beaufort County Courthouse, built in 1786, was the scene of a sermon preached by what famous circuit riding evangelist?

A. Bishop Francis Asbury, first Methodist bishop in America.

Q. Who was the well-known free black cabinetmaker of the mid-1800s in Milton?

A. Tom Day.

Q. What college traces its roots to 1857, when it was established as Charlotte Female Institute?

A. Queens College.

Q. At what location did Loyalists and patriots first clash on February 27, 1776?

A. The Battle at Moores Creek Bridge.

Q. The graves of Arthur Dobbs (Royal Governor, 1754–1765), Benjamin Smith (governor, 1810–1811), and United States Supreme Court Justice Alfred Moore lie in which county?

A. Brunswick.

Q. The oldest brick house in North Carolina, the Newbold-White House, located southeast of Hertford, was built in what year?

A. 1685.

———◆———

Q. In what year did the North Carolina legislature first cede the state's western lands to the United States Government, although it later tried to withdraw its action?

A. 1784.

———◆———

Q. A state-sponsored specialty school was opened in Raleigh in 1845 to educate what type of handicapped persons?

A. The deaf.

———◆———

Q. Fort Bragg was named for what Civil War hero?

A. Braxton Bragg, Confederate Army general.

———◆———

Q. What is the oldest continually operating cotton mill in North Carolina?

A. Rocky Mount Mills.

———◆———

Q. According to the 1860 census, how many colleges did North Carolina have?

A. Sixteen.

———◆———

Q. Under the Stamp Act enacted in 1765 by the British Parliament, how many tax stamps were sold in North Carolina?

A. None.

Q. The city of Charlotte elected its first black mayor, Harvey Gantt, in what year?

A. 1985.

◆

Q. Who served as lieutenant governor of the first English colony on Roanoke Island?

A. Ralph Lane.

◆

Q. Dolley Payne Madison, wife of President James Madison, was born in what North Carolina county?

A. Guilford.

◆

Q. What artist produced the silversmith work and engraving of the North Carolina state seal?

A. William Tisdale, New Bern.

◆

Q. What Brunswick County fort was the first fortification authorized by the North Carolina legislature?

A. Fort Johnson.

◆

Q. On what date did North Carolina gain statehood?

A. November 21, 1789.

◆

Q. In what year did a hurricane open the Hatteras and Oregon inlets off Portsmouth Island and change the shipping patterns?

A. 1846.

Q. North Carolina's Juanita M. Kreps served the Carter administration in what capacity?

A. Secretary of Commerce and Labor.

———◆———

Q. What was the name of the first steamboat built in North Carolina?

A. *Prometheus*, 1818.

———◆———

Q. The Greene County Courthouse, erected during the Great Depression, was designed by what government agency?

A. The Works Progress Administration (WPA).

———◆———

Q. What governor of North Carolina in 1799 resigned to become Minister Plenipotentiary to France?

A. William R. Davie.

———◆———

Q. Where did the first recorded Protestant baptismal service take place in the New World?

A. The "Lost Colony" on Roanoke Island.

———◆———

Q. In what museum can you view the original Carolina Charter document?

A. The North Carolina Museum of History, Raleigh.

———◆———

Q. What breathtakingly beautiful Georgian building served as North Carolina's first state capitol upon its completion in 1770?

A. Tryon Palace, New Bern.

Q. Who originally headed the Warrenton Academy?

A. Marcus George.

———◆———

Q. What early statesman was referred to as the "Father of Religious Liberty in North Carolina"?

A. William Gaston.

———◆———

Q. The first public reading of the Declaration of Independence in North Carolina was given by Cornelius Harnett at what county courthouse?

A. The Halifax County Courthouse.

———◆———

Q. Where was the first hospital for mentally ill blacks in the nation established in 1884?

A. Goldsboro.

———◆———

Q. The housewarming at the opening of the Biltmore mansion in 1895 centered around what holiday?

A. Christmas.

———◆———

Q. Who founded the only private mint in the southeastern United States near Rutherfordton in 1831?

A. Christopher Bechtler.

———◆———

Q. On March 8, 1705, what settlement became the first town incorporated by the North Carolina assembly?

A. Bath.

Q. What marshland in northeastern North Carolina was used as a hideaway by outlaws and escaped slaves?

A. The Great Dismal Swamp.

———◆———

Q. What Marion resident was the only survivor of the Battle of Little Big Horn?

A. Dan Kanipe.

———◆———

Q. What religious group sponsored North Carolina College at Mount Pleasant in 1851?

A. The Lutherans.

———◆———

Q. Who was the first known permanent white settler in North Carolina?

A. Nathaniel Batts, 1657.

———◆———

Q. What organization led the people of the colony of North Carolina in opposing the British Stamp Act of 1765?

A. The Sons of Liberty.

———◆———

Q. The founder of the New York *Tribune,* Horace Greeley, married a teacher in what North Carolina community?

A. Warrenton.

———◆———

Q. Who is said to be the "father of Raleigh and of Wake County"?

A. Joel Lane.

Q. What law passed in 1974 gave the state authority over the development of land on the North Carolina coast?

A. The Coastal Carolina Land Management Act.

———◆———

Q. The resting place of which Civil War ironclad, situated off Cape Hatteras, was chosen as the nation's first underwater National Register and Marine Sanctuary?

A. U.S.S. *Monitor*.

———◆———

Q. What name was given to the highly debated 1965 cultural arts and education bill?

A. The "toe-dancing bill."

———◆———

Q. A Spanish expedition led by what explorer reached Currituck in 1566?

A. Pedro de Coronas.

———◆———

Q. By 1775 what was the estimated number of beef cattle being exported from North Carolina?

A. 50,000 head annually.

———◆———

Q. Who led the meeting at New Bern in 1774 to elect delegates to represent North Carolina in the Continental Congress?

A. John Harvey.

———◆———

Q. Saint Thomas Episcopal Church in Bath houses what artifacts given to the church by King George II in 1740?

A. A 1704 Bible and candlesticks.

Q. What name was given to the first school bus in the state, which began operation in 1917?

A. "Benzine Buggy."

———◆———

Q. By 1910 what North Carolina-based company was the biggest manufacturer of cotton hosiery?

A. Durham Hosiery Company.

———◆———

Q. Whose initials are etched into handmade bricks on the Governor's Mansion?

A. Convicts who helped build and complete the mansion in 1891.

———◆———

Q. Guilford College, established in 1837 by the Society of Friends (Quakers), would not allow what activity on campus until 1887, because of their puritanical beliefs?

A. Singing.

———◆———

Q. What was the principal Quaker town of the eighteenth and nineteenth centuries?

A. Jamestown.

———◆———

Q. In 1540 what Spanish explorer sought gold in the present-day counties of Jackson, Macon, Clay, and Cherokee?

A. Hernando de Soto.

———◆———

Q. Who commissioned the Biltmore mansion to be built as his private residence?

A. George Washington Vanderbilt.

Q. In what year was the Biltmore mansion featured on a United States postage stamp?

A. 1981.

———◆———

Q. What twelve-year-old North Carolina boy in 1799 discovered the first gold nugget in the nation?

A. Conrad Reed.

———◆———

Q. What governor began to improve North Carolina's public education system in 1901?

A. Charles B. Aycock, 1901–1905.

———◆———

Q. During the War Between the States, how many successful runs were made to Nassau by North Carolina blockade-runners?

A. 365.

———◆———

Q. Who was the Royal Navy officer who on November 22, 1718, killed Blackbeard the pirate during a battle near Ocracoke Inlet?

A. Lieutenant Robert Maynard.

———◆———

Q. Who were the first Indians from North Carolina to visit England in 1584?

A. Wanchese and Manteo.

———◆———

Q. Why was Fontana Dam built?

A. To give power to factories manufacturing goods for the war effort during World War II.

Q. What mysterious word was found carved on a tree at the site of the "Lost Colony" by a relief expedition in 1590?

A. *Croatoan.*

◆

Q. What 1765 law so angered citizens of Brunswick that they took up arms to oust the officials in charge of the tax?

A. The Stamp Act.

◆

Q. Who was the first North Carolina governor elected by popular vote?

A. E. B. Dudley.

◆

Q. What college was founded in Newton in 1851?

A. Catawba College.

◆

Q. Fayetteville native J. N. Maffitt was reputed to be the best at what Civil War occupation?

A. Blockade runner.

◆

Q. Where was the first sit-in demonstration in 1960, protesting segregation?

A. The lunch counter of the F. W. Woolworth Store, Greensboro.

◆

Q. What was the name of the first fort built on Roanoke Island?

A. Fort Raleigh.

Q. What three delegates from North Carolina signed the Declaration of Independence?

A. Joseph Hewes, William Hooper, and John Penn.

———◆———

Q. Who was the convicted ax murderess who in 1833 at Morganton became the first woman to be executed by hanging in North Carolina?

A. Frankie Silvers.

———◆———

Q. Work on the Blue Ridge Parkway began in what year?

A. 1935.

———◆———

Q. What college was the first institution of higher learning chartered for women in North Carolina?

A. Greensboro College, 1838.

———◆———

Q. In the early eighteenth century, what religious entity was established as North Carolina's official church?

A. The Anglican Church.

———◆———

Q. What Indian uprising that began on September 22, 1711, took the lives of hundreds of white settlers?

A. The Tuscarora War.

———◆———

Q. What former North Carolina senator claimed that he was the first to measure Mount Mitchell and not Dr. Elisha Mitchell?

A. Thomas L. Clingman.

Q. In what year was television introduced to North Carolina?

A. 1949.

———◆———

Q. What present-day lighthouse stands on the site of the state's first lighthouse built in 1796?

A. Bald Head Island Lighthouse, 1817.

———◆———

Q. What North Carolina battleground was the first in the nation to be designated a national military park?

A. Guilford Courthouse National Military Park.

———◆———

Q. Who was North Carolina's only governor to be removed from office by impeachment?

A. William Holden, 1871.

———◆———

Q. What two airborne divisions were trained at Fort Bragg during World War II?

A. The 82nd and the 101st.

———◆———

Q. When did English colonists arrive on Roanoke Island, establishing England's first New World colony?

A. August 17, 1585.

———◆———

Q. What Spanish explorer led an expedition to the North Carolina area in July of 1526 in an attempt to establish a colony?

A. Lucas Vásquez de Ayllón.

Q. What North Carolina coastal fortification is considered one of the finest examples of nineteenth-century military architecture?

A. Fort Macon.

———◆———

Q. The transaction between George Durant and which Yeopim Indian leader on March 1, 1662, stands as the oldest recorded land grant in North Carolina?

A. King Kilcocanen.

———◆———

Q. What North Carolinian was appointed by George Washington to the first United States Supreme Court in 1790?

A. James Iredell.

———◆———

Q. Money was appropriated in 1754 for the establishment of what type of public institution in the colony?

A. Public schools.

———◆———

Q. What carpetbagger politician was assassinated by the Ku Klux Klan in the Caswell County Courthouse?

A. Senator John ("Chicken") Stephens.

———◆———

Q. What federal document did the state legislature unanimously ratify in 1778?

A. The Articles of Confederation.

———◆———

Q. Who is known as the "father of the University of North Carolina"?

A. William R. Davie.

Q. How did North Carolina rank chronologically in joining the Union?

A. Twelfth.

❖

Q. What was Blackbeard's actual name?

A. Edward Teach.

❖

Q. In 1972, who was the first Republican elected governor of North Carolina since 1896?

A. James E. Holshouser, Jr.

❖

Q. North Carolina was the first colony to instruct its delegates to vote for what movement?

A. Independence.

❖

Q. What patriot was called the "Samuel Adams of North Carolina"?

A. Cornelius Harnett.

❖

Q. Who was the secretary of the Confederate treasury who tried to persuade Jefferson Davis to relocate the Confederate capital from Richmond, Virginia, to Flat Rock?

A. Christopher Gustavus Memminger.

❖

Q. Hugh Waddell of Wilmington was a hero of what war?

A. The French and Indian War, 1754–1763.

Q. What name did the English bestow upon present-day North Carolina and adjoining coastal lands in 1584 in honor of the unmarried Queen Elizabeth?

A. Virginia.

———◆———

Q. What dwelling is the oldest standing structure in Mecklenburg County?

A. The Hezekiah Alexander Homesite, 1774.

———◆———

Q. The Fayetteville and Western plank road, the world's longest, extended for a total of how many miles?

A. 129.

———◆———

Q. How many militiamen did North Carolina provide during the War of 1812?

A. 14,000.

———◆———

Q. Who introduced an ordinance for secession of North Carolina from the Union on May 20, 1861?

A. Burton Craige.

———◆———

Q. Edenton was incorporated as a town in what year?

A. 1722.

———◆———

Q. Where did the Reverend Joseph Pilmore deliver the first Methodist sermon in North Carolina on September 12, 1772?

A. The Currituck Courthouse.

Q. What railroad line, running between Marion and Erwin, Tennessee, completed in 1908, is considered to be the greatest engineering feat and the curviest section of line in the eastern United States?

A. The Clinchfield Railroad.

◆

Q. Winston-Salem State University was the first black institution in the nation to grant what degree?

A. A degree to teach elementary education.

◆

Q. Who was the first governor to occupy the present-day Executive Mansion?

A. Daniel G. Fowle, 1889–1891.

◆

Q. What mode of public transportation was established in the state in 1789?

A. A stagecoach line.

◆

Q. What Williamsboro church has the distinction of being the oldest frame church in North Carolina?

A. Saint John's Episcopal.

◆

Q. What erroneous name has often been given to the State Constitution of 1868?

A. "The Canby Constitution."

◆

Q. What colonial architect designed and built Tryon Palace?

A. John Hawks.

Q. What battle gave Union forces a stronghold in mainland North Carolina?

A. The Battle of New Bern, 1862.

———◆———

Q. Before the War Between the States, North Carolina was the nation's leading producer of what beverage?

A. Wine.

———◆———

Q. Who in 1712 became the first governor in charge of the northern part of Carolina?

A. Edward Hyde.

———◆———

Q. The first cotton mill in the South, The Schenck-Warlick Mill, was built near what community around 1813?

A. Lincolnton.

———◆———

Q. What church has the oldest charter in the state?

A. Saint Paul's Episcopal Church, organized in 1701.

———◆———

Q. Where was the Mordecai Female Seminary founded?

A. Warrenton.

———◆———

Q. At what convention on November 21, 1789, did the North Carolina legislature ratify the United States Constitution?

A. The Fayetteville Convention.

Q. Where may Spanish inscriptions believed to date back to de Soto's 1540 expedition be seen?

A. Whiteside Mountain.

———◆———

Q. What is the oldest surviving artificial canal in the nation?

A. The Dismal Swamp Canal, dug after 1790.

———◆———

Q. Who was the first recorded European to explore the coast of North Carolina?

A. Giovanni da Verrazzano, 1524.

———◆———

Q. What Glendale Springs attraction is sponsored by the Northwest Development Association to keep more than 260 handicrafts alive?

A. Northwest Trading Post.

———◆———

Q. What railroad line did General Robert E. Lee call the "lifeline of the Confederacy"?

A. The Wilmington and Weldon Railroad.

———◆———

Q. What nickname was applied to North Carolina in the early 1800s due to its unprogressive character?

A. The "Rip Van Winkle" state.

———◆———

Q. What company in 1888 became the first furniture manufacturer in North Carolina?

A. The High Point Furniture Company.

Q. Who was the advertising genius known for making Bull Durham tobacco famous in the nineteenth century?

A. Jule Korner.

———◆———

Q. What Brunswick County planter commanded the militia that burned Fort Johnston on July 18, 1775?

A. Robert Howe.

———◆———

Q. What port served as the main Confederate center of blockade-running during the War Between the States?

A. The port of Wilmington.

———◆———

Q. North Carolina established what agency in 1925 to oversee the state's natural resources?

A. The Department of Conservation and Development.

———◆———

Q. What college was founded in 1802 by the Moravians?

A. Salem College.

———◆———

Q. How many cotton mills did North Carolina have in 1900?

A. 177.

———◆———

Q. How many towns with 1,000 or more population did North Carolina have in 1820?

A. Six.

Q. What group met at Charlotte in May, 1775, to issue a formal declaration of North Carolina's disregard of British sovereignty?

A. Mecklenburg County Safety Committee.

------◆------

Q. What fort served the Confederacy as its largest earthwork fortification?

A. Fort Fisher, Kure Beach.

------◆------

Q. Who were the first two explorers to visit Roanoke Island in 1584 for England under the authority of Sir Walter Raleigh?

A. Captain Philip Amadas and Arthur Barlowe.

------◆------

Q. What political organization was active among blacks during the Reconstruction Period?

A. The Union League.

------◆------

Q. How many surplus Confederate uniforms did North Carolina's warehouses contain at the close of the War Between the States?

A. 92,000.

------◆------

Q. The hull of what Confederate ironclad ram boat was constructed near the junction of present-day U.S. Highway 258 and the Roanoke River?

A. The *Albemarle*.

------◆------

Q. Who in 1705 became the first recorded professional teacher in the colony?

A. Charles Griffin.

HISTORY

Q. By what name was the fight concerning the Established Church within the early colony known?

A. The Cary Rebellion.

———◆———

Q. How many miles of railroad track did North Carolina have in 1860?

A. 391.

———◆———

Q. What famous gun designer was born north of Murfreesboro in Hertford County on September 12, 1818?

A. Richard J. Gatling.

———◆———

Q. Who was the governor in 1949 who implemented a "Go Forward" program for North Carolina?

A. W. Kerr Scott.

———◆———

Q. North Carolina led the nation in the production of what type of goods for use by the Quartermaster Corps during World War II?

A. Textile goods.

———◆———

Q. What four crimes were defined as capital offenses under the State Constitution of 1868?

A. Arson, burglary, murder, and rape.

———◆———

Q. Whose forces defeated General Joseph E. Johnston's Confederate forces at Bentonville?

A. General William T. Sherman's army.

—92—

Q. By 1789 the North Carolina legislature had created how many counties in what would become the state of Tennessee?

A. Seven counties: Davidson, Hawkins, Greene, Sullivan, Sumner, Tennessee, and Washington.

———◆———

Q. What political party became the driving force among North Carolina farmers during the late 1880s and early 1890s?

A. The Peoples Party (Populist).

———◆———

Q. At what home near Rich Square did Quakers maintain a station in the underground railroad for runaway slaves?

A. The William Copeland House.

———◆———

Q. What museum contains such unique items as a watch fob made from the first Atlantic cable, dressed fleas, and an eight-legged pig?

A. Bellhaven Memorial Museum.

———◆———

Q. The Quakers opened what school in 1837 that evolved into Guilford College?

A. New Garden Boarding School.

———◆———

Q. What state institution opened in Raleigh in 1856?

A. The State Hospital for the Insane.

———◆———

Q. Who was the Edgecombe County representative to the General Assembly who died of fever in Vera Cruz during the Mexican War?

A. Colonel Louis D. Wilson.

Q. What was the fate of the Diamond Shoals Lightship on August 8, 1918?

A. She was sunk by a German U-boat.

———◆———

Q. North Carolina entered the Union too late to vote for which president?

A. George Washington.

———◆———

Q. What percentage of North Carolina families held slaves in 1790?

A. Thirty-one.

———◆———

Q. What community was the site of North Carolina's first free rural mail delivery in 1896?

A. The China Grove community, Rowan County.

———◆———

Q. In December of 1775, what Currituck girl rode her pony all night, covering fifty miles, to deliver an important message to General William Skinner?

A. Betsy Dowdy.

———◆———

Q. What items were used to make pontoons to provide a floating bridge across the broad Perquimans River near Hertford in 1784?

A. Whiskey barrels.

———◆———

Q. Under the State Constitution of 1868, what length of term was established for governors?

A. A four-year term.

Q. What type of road was constructed in 1738–1739 from New England to Charleston, permitting the first regular mail service to North Carolina?

A. Post road.

———◆———

Q. Where on March 18, 1861, was the Confederate "Stars and Bars" flag first displayed?

A. Louisburg.

———◆———

Q. By 1900, what was the average number of days per year that public schools were open in North Carolina?

A. Approximately seventy.

———◆———

Q. To what company in 1904 was the Atlantic and North Carolina Railroad leased for ninety-one years?

A. The Howland Improvement Company.

———◆———

Q. What county courthouse was burned by a determined court clerk in 1878?

A. The Lenoir County Courthouse.

———◆———

Q. Who built the first drawbridge in North Carolina and possibly in the United States?

A. Benjamin Heron (over the Northeast Cape Fear River).

———◆———

Q. What nickname did Governor Cameron Morrison receive?

A. "Good Roads Governor."

Q. What organization was formed by farmers in 1768 to combat corruption in local government?

A. The Regulators.

———◆———

Q. Which was North Carolina's most politically powerful newspaper during the first half of the nineteenth century?

A. The *Raleigh Register*.

———◆———

Q. Due to excessive inflation and shortages, to what price did coffee soar in North Carolina by the end of the War Between the States?

A. $100 per pound.

———◆———

Q. Who founded the first Baptist church, Chowan Church, in 1727 near present-day Cisco?

A. The Reverend Paul Palmer.

———◆———

Q. When was North Carolina readmitted to the Union?

A. July 20, 1868.

———◆———

Q. What was the largest and bloodiest battle fought on North Carolina soil during the War Between the States?

A. The Battle of Bentonville, March 20–21, 1865.

———◆———

Q. A branch of what federal agency was opened in Charlotte in 1837?

A. The United States mint.

Q. Who was the first constitutionally elected governor?

A. Richard Caswell, 1776–1780, 1784–1787.

———◆———

Q. What United States president owned a portion of the Dismal Swamp and is said to have shoveled out the first bit of dirt for the Dismal Swamp Canal?

A. George Washington.

———◆———

Q. How much capital investment was wiped out in North Carolina by the abolition of slavery?

A. Two hundred million dollars.

———◆———

Q. Though chartered in 1789, in what year did the University of North Carolina open its doors to students?

A. 1795.

———◆———

Q. At 161½ miles, what North Carolina railroad was the longest in the world when it was completed on March 7, 1840?

A. Wilmington and Weldon Railroad.

———◆———

Q. What memorial was erected on top of Kill Devil Hill by the federal government in 1932?

A. The Wright Brothers National Memorial.

———◆———

Q. What form of public transportation began service in Asheville in 1889?

A. Electric street cars.

Q. Who was North Carolina's colorful governor during the War Between the States?

A. Zebulon Vance, 1862–1865.

———◆———

Q. For what purpose were the large boulders on either side of the entrance to the Davidson County Courthouse used prior to the War Between the States?

A. To exhibit slaves to be sold at auction.

———◆———

Q. What request did President Abraham Lincoln make of North Carolina on April 15, 1861, in response to the southern "insurrection"?

A. A request for two regiments of men.

———◆———

Q. During World War II what North Carolina installation became the Army's most comprehensive facility?

A. Fort Bragg.

———◆———

Q. What national farm organization established a branch in North Carolina in 1875?

A. The Grange.

———◆———

Q. What was the name of the notorious stagecoach inn built about 1800 on the Virginia–North Carolina line near present-day U.S. Highway 17?

A. The Halfway House.

———◆———

Q. In what county was a reservation for the Tuscarora Indians established in 1717?

A. Bertie.

Q. On whose farm was bright leaf tobacco accidentally processed for the first time in 1852?

A. Captain Abisha Salde, Yanceyville.

◆

Q. William Dorsey Pender, who was killed at Gettysburg and is buried in Tarboro, held what Confederate Army record?

A. The youngest major general.

◆

Q. Where was the first state agricultural fair held in 1853?

A. Raleigh.

◆

Q. What was the name of the college founded about 1838 that later became Duke University?

A. Trinity College.

◆

Q. How many North Carolina soldiers died during the War Between the States due to battle losses and disease?

A. 40,275.

◆

Q. Who, along with his five Coast Guard crewmen, rescued forty-two persons from a torpedoed British tanker off Hatteras Island on August 16, 1918?

A. Captain John Allen Midgett.

◆

Q. What Dunn native and World War II hero was known as the "father of the Airborne"?

A. Gen. William C. Lee.

Q. Who took military command of state government on April 29, 1865?

A. Gen. John Schofield.

———◆———

Q. According to the 1820 census, New Bern was the largest town in North Carolina with how many residents?

A. 3,663.

———◆———

Q. How many North Carolinians served in the military during World War I?

A. 86,457.

———◆———

Q. What North Carolina textile giant was founded in 1923?

A. Burlington Mills.

———◆———

Q. How many dollars worth of war bonds were purchased by the residents of North Carolina during World War I?

A. Sixty million dollars.

———◆———

Q. Where in North Carolina were the first telephone systems put into operation in 1879?

A. Raleigh and Wilmington.

———◆———

Q. What federal document did North Carolina fail to ratify at the 1788 Hillsboro Convention?

A. The Constitution of the United States.

Q. By what name was Chapel Hill first known?

A. New Hope Chapel.

———◆———

Q. Who was appointed provisional governor of North Carolina by President Andrew Johnson in May, 1865?

A. William W. Holden.

———◆———

Q. How many North Carolinians served as Confederate soldiers during the War Between the States?

A. Approximately 125,000.

———◆———

Q. What fort at the mouth of Cape Fear was nicknamed the "Gibraltar of America"?

A. Fort Fisher.

———◆———

Q. In what county was the first public school for blacks in North Carolina?

A. Craven.

———◆———

Q. What was the name of the first college in North Carolina, operating in Charlotte between 1771 and 1780?

A. Queen's College.

———◆———

Q. By 1880 what portion of farms in North Carolina were operated by tenant farmers?

A. One-third.

Q. Who sewed the original "Stars and Bars" Confederate flag?

A. Rebecca M. Winborne.

———◆———

Q. What federal agency provided $1,500,000 worth of food and clothing to North Carolina's freed slave population during the Reconstruction period?

A. The Freedman's Bureau.

———◆———

Q. What two railroads opened for business in North Carolina in 1840?

A. The Wilmington and Raleigh and the Raleigh and Gaston.

———◆———

Q. By what name did small tenant farmers become known following the War Between the States?

A. Sharecroppers.

———◆———

Q. Under whose leadership was the Farmers Alliance organized in North Carolina in 1887?

A. Leonidas L. Polk.

———◆———

Q. On what type of foundation was the Martin County courthouse built in 1774?

A. Stilts over the Roanoke River.

———◆———

Q. Who established the Rocky Mount Cotton Mills in 1818?

A. Joel Battle.

Q. What agricultural organization was formed in Raleigh in 1852?

A. The State Agricultural Society.

———◆———

Q. By the appointment of the Assembly in 1749, who became the first printer in the colony?

A. James Davis.

———◆———

Q. Who was the first president of the University of North Carolina?

A. Joseph Caldwell.

———◆———

Q. What was the only fortification built in the colony during the French and Indian War?

A. Fort Dobbs.

———◆———

Q. To help stimulate rural power line construction, North Carolina established what agency in 1935?

A. The North Carolina Rural Electrification Authority.

———◆———

Q. What Methodist-sponsored school was founded in Lenoir in 1858?

A. Davenport Female College.

———◆———

Q. The wreck of what ship near Nags Head on November 24, 1877, took 108 lives?

A. The *Huron*.

Q. In what county was the first postal service in North Carolina established?

A. Craven.

———◆———

Q. Whom did Zebulon B. Vance defeat in 1876, thereby regaining Democratic control of the governorship?

A. Thomas Settle.

———◆———

Q. What railroad system was established in North Carolina in 1906?

A. The Norfolk and Southern Railway Company.

———◆———

Q. What association of Separate Baptist churches was formed in 1758?

A. The Big Sandy Association.

———◆———

Q. Rodanthe on Hatteras Island is locally called by what name?

A. Chicamacomico, after a former Coast Guard station.

———◆———

Q. By 1850 how many "common" or public schools were there in North Carolina?

A. 2,657.

———◆———

Q. Who attempted to have the statehouse burned in Raleigh to cover up fraudulent land grants of the 1790s?

A. James Glasgow.

ARTS & LITERATURE

C H A P T E R   F O U R

Q. What Harnett County native is known as the father of outdoor drama?

A. Paul Green.

———◆———

Q. What North Carolina author has reportedly sold more books than any other in the state?

A. Billy Graham.

———◆———

Q. What is the state song?

A. "The Old North State."

———◆———

Q. What landscape artist designed the grounds of the Biltmore mansion?

A. Frederick Law Olmsted, who also designed Central Park in New York City.

———◆———

Q. What North Carolina author was known for his stories and novels about the mystical troubadour Silver John?

A. Manly Wade Wellman.

Q. What artist sculpted the statue of Sir Walter Raleigh that stands in the state's capitol?

A. Bruno Lucchesi.

◆

Q. Author/journalist Tom Wicker was born in what community?

A. Hamlet.

◆

Q. Beginning in 1921, what North Carolina author was the only American writer on the staff of a London paper?

A. Phillips Russell.

◆

Q. What was the pen name of Salisbury-born Francis Fisher who wrote many light romance novels?

A. Christian Reid.

◆

Q. *The Impending Crisis of the South: How to Meet It* by Hinton Rowan Helper of Davie County was a great influence leading to what historical event?

A. The War Between the States.

◆

Q. Greensboro is the home of what museum noted for having one of the nation's best collections of African art?

A. The African Heritage Museum.

◆

Q. In what city was Allan Gurganus, author of *The Oldest Living Confederate Widow Tells All,* born?

A. Rocky Mount.

Q. *The Tall Woman,* a novel that depicts the life of a courageous mountain woman, was written by what renowned Asheville-born author?

A. Wilma Dykeman.

———◆———

Q. What architect designed the Biltmore mansion?

A. Richard Morris Hunt.

———◆———

Q. North Carolina playwright Paul Green won what award for his first play, *In Abraham's Bosom?*

A. Pulitzer Prize, 1927.

———◆———

Q. The world's largest painting, a cyclorama of the Battle of Gettysburg, is stored in what city?

A. Winston-Salem.

———◆———

Q. What product of Seagrove in Randolph County has gained worldwide fame and is on permanent display at the Smithsonian Institution?

A. Pottery.

———◆———

Q. In 1700 Bath became the first community to provide what public facility?

A. A public library.

———◆———

Q. Who has authored several guidebooks about the historical and architectural landmarks of North Carolina?

A. Marguerite Schumann.

Q. What town was the birthplace of Thomas Wolfe?

A. Asheville.

◆

Q. What school houses the beginnings of the Dizzy Gillespie Jazz Hall of Fame?

A. Laurinburg Institute, where Dizzy graduated in 1935.

◆

Q. What was Kaye Gibbons's first novel?

A. *Ellen Foster.*

◆

Q. *North Carolina Miscellany,* 1966, is a collection of interesting and unusual information on places, people, and folklore written by which author?

A. Richard Walser.

◆

Q. What state music festival was organized in Asheville in 1928?

A. American Folk Festival–Mountain Dance and Folk Festival.

◆

Q. The Malcolm Blue Historic Crafts and Skills Festival is held in what town?

A. Aberdeen.

◆

Q. Educators Barbara and Thomas Parramore authored what North Carolina textbooks?

A. *The People of North Carolina* and *Carolina Quest.*

Q. What city houses America's first state art museum?

A. Raleigh.

———◆———

Q. What is the title of the famous short story that Marjorie Kinnan Rawlings wrote while living at Banner Elk?

A. "Mother in Manville."

———◆———

Q. What town is the birthplace of Pulitzer-prize-winning playwright, Paul Green?

A. Lillington.

———◆———

Q. What Davie County-born native is known for his volumes on North Carolina history?

A. Dr. Hugh T. Lefler.

———◆———

Q. Internationally known architect Rafael Guastavino built what Asheville church?

A. The Catholic Church of Saint Lawrence.

———◆———

Q. What famous pianist included in his last concerto bird songs he had heard sung at his window while visiting a health resort in Asheville?

A. Béla Bartók.

———◆———

Q. What is the title of the biography of football great Charlie Justice written by Julian W. Scheer?

A. *Choo Choo.*

Q. "Frankie Silvers Ballad," composed in the Morganton jail in 1833, evolved into what popular twentieth-century ballad?

A. "Frankie & Johnny."

———◆———

Q. What Winston-Salem artist was commissioned to paint portraits of President Richard Nixon, Queen Elizabeth, and the royalty of Saudi Arabia?

A. Joe King.

———◆———

Q. What North Carolina-born writer began his literary career in prison?

A. William Sydney Porter (O. Henry).

———◆———

Q. What is the title of the autobiographical memoir that Carl Sandburg wrote while living in North Carolina?

A. *Always the Young Stranger*.

———◆———

Q. A building is named for the Poet Laureate of North Carolina, James Larkin Pearson, on what college campus?

A. Wilkes Community College.

———◆———

Q. What was the name of the plantation north of Clarkton where Whistler's mother lived for a time before moving to Paris where her son painted her famous portrait?

A. Oak Forest.

———◆———

Q. The architects of the Empire State Building, Shreve and Lamb of New York City, designed what great example of 1920s Art Deco-style architecture in Winston-Salem?

A. The R. J. Reynolds Office Building.

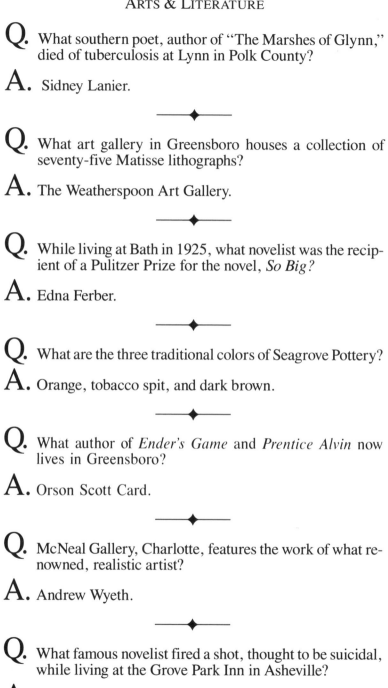

Q. What southern poet, author of "The Marshes of Glynn," died of tuberculosis at Lynn in Polk County?

A. Sidney Lanier.

◆

Q. What art gallery in Greensboro houses a collection of seventy-five Matisse lithographs?

A. The Weatherspoon Art Gallery.

◆

Q. While living at Bath in 1925, what novelist was the recipient of a Pulitzer Prize for the novel, *So Big?*

A. Edna Ferber.

◆

Q. What are the three traditional colors of Seagrove Pottery?

A. Orange, tobacco spit, and dark brown.

◆

Q. What author of *Ender's Game* and *Prentice Alvin* now lives in Greensboro?

A. Orson Scott Card.

◆

Q. McNeal Gallery, Charlotte, features the work of what renowned, realistic artist?

A. Andrew Wyeth.

◆

Q. What famous novelist fired a shot, thought to be suicidal, while living at the Grove Park Inn in Asheville?

A. F. Scott Fitzgerald.

Q. What was the title of the historical novel that Carl Sandburg wrote while living in North Carolina?

A. *Remembrance Rock.*

---◆---

Q. Statesville-born fresco painter Ben Long, noted for his works at Saint Mary's and Holy Trinity churches in Ashe County, received what prestigious international award?

A. The Leonardo da Vinci International Art Award.

---◆---

Q. Where is the Onslow County Museum Arts and Crafts Festival held?

A. Richlands.

---◆---

Q. Brevard is known worldwide for what contribution to the arts?

A. The Brevard Music Center.

---◆---

Q. What theatrical company is the only resident professional equity theater in North Carolina?

A. ACE–Charlotte's Repertory Theatre.

---◆---

Q. What author is credited with writing the first North Carolina book, published in 1588?

A. Thomas Hariott.

---◆---

Q. What Chapel Hill writer and publisher of supernatural fiction was once a resident in psychiatry at John Unstead Hospital?

A. Karl Edward Wagner.

Q. *Dred: A Tale of the Great Dismal Swamp*, was written by what renowned author who considered this her best work?

A. Harriet Beecher Stowe.

Q. What novel was written by James Boyd while living in Southern Pines?

A. *Drums*, 1925.

Q. Under what pseudonym has Tom Wicker written?

A. Paul Connolly.

Q. Burnsville is the home of what summer theater operated by the University of North Carolina at Greensboro?

A. Parkway Playhouse.

Q. What university, the third largest private university in the state, is in Bluies Creek?

A. Campbell University.

Q. What farm publication was established by Leonidas L. Polk?

A. The *Progressive Farmer*.

Q. Recipient of many awards, author Reynolds Price has long been associated with what university?

A. Duke University.

Q. Where was short story author O. Henry born?

A. Guilford County.

———◆———

Q. The library at Fayetteville State University was named for what black novelist, one of the first in the nation?

A. Charles Waddell Chesnutt.

———◆———

Q. What author wrote *A History of a Small Place*?

A. T. R. Pearson.

———◆———

Q. Carson McCullers finished her first novel, *The Heart Is a Lonely Hunter*, while living with her husband in what North Carolina community?

A. Fayetteville.

———◆———

Q. Who authored the popular history of the War of 1812, *Poltroons and Patriots*, 1954?

A. Glenn Tucker.

———◆———

Q. As director of the Carolina Playmakers at Chapel Hill, what professor influenced such writers as Paul Green, Thomas Wolfe, and Francis Gray Patton?

A. Frederick H. Koch.

———◆———

Q. Where is the Mountaineer Book Fair held?

A. Macon County Public Library, Franklin.

Q. What Thomas Wolfe autobiographical novel stunned and offended people of his hometown?

A. *Look Homeward, Angel,* 1929.

———◆———

Q. Harry Golden authored what book that was turned into a Broadway play and then sold over a million copies in paperback?

A. *Only in America.*

———◆———

Q. What award-winning juvenile book written by Julia Montgomery Street tells of mountain people around the Toe River area of Mitchell County?

A. *Fiddlers Fancy.*

———◆———

Q. Tom Wicker became the associate editor of what widely read newspaper in 1968?

A. The *New York Times.*

———◆———

Q. Who authored *The Clansman,* which was made into a successful stage play in 1905?

A. Thomas Dixon, Jr.

———◆———

Q. Alexander Key of Franklin wrote what 1968 science fiction book for juveniles that was later made into a Walt Disney movie?

A. *Escape to Witch Mountain.*

———◆———

Q. Who authored the outdoor drama *Unto These Hills* which he wrote for his master's thesis at the University of North Carolina at Chapel Hill?

A. Kermit Hunter.

Q. Where is the International Folk Festival held?

A. Fayetteville.

———◆———

Q. What pamphlet was the first major abolitionist statement written by a black American, Wilmington native David Walker?

A. *Appeal to the Coloured Citizens of the World* (1829).

———◆———

Q. What playhouse was named the State Theatre of North Carolina in 1961?

A. The Flat Rock Playhouse.

———◆———

Q. What city hall is considered the finest example of Richardson Romanesque in the United States?

A. Statesville.

———◆———

Q. Edna Ferber wrote what 1926 best seller telling the stories of people she met at the John Adams Floating Theater in Bath?

A. *Showboat.*

———◆———

Q. On whose press was the first newspaper, first pamphlet, and first book printed in North Carolina?

A. James Davis, New Bern.

———◆———

Q. Who sculpted the equestrian statue of R. J. Reynolds that stands at the Forsyth County Hall of Justice?

A. Earlene Heath King.

Q. James Boyd wrote what novel describing Lower Cape Fear country at the time of the War Between the States?

A. *Marching On*, 1927.

———◆———

Q. What famous craft school, established in a single building in 1923, now occupies thirty-three buildings, employs a staff of seventy, and is said to be America's largest?

A. Penland School of Crafts.

———◆———

Q. Fayetteville lawyer Robert Strange authored what 1839 historical novel describing the unfair treatment of the Cherokee Indians by whites?

A. *Eoneguski*, or *The Cherokee Chief*.

———◆———

Q. What early North Carolina governor became known for his patriotic poems?

A. Thomas Burke.

———◆———

Q. Historical musical instruments are made by craftsman George Kelischek in which community?

A. Brasstown.

———◆———

Q. Raleigh-born Frances Gray Patton penned what award-winning 1954 novel later made into a motion picture?

A. *Good Morning, Miss Dove*.

———◆———

Q. In what part of the state did potters from Staffordshire, England, settle in the 1700s?

A. The Sandhills area.

Q. Whose former residence now houses the Museum of American Art in Winston-Salem?

A. R. J. Reynolds, Reynolds House.

———◆———

Q. What North Carolina poet is buried at the old Spring Hill Cemetery in Scotland County?

A. John Charles McNeill.

———◆———

Q. Sherwood Anderson was a guest in what North Carolina home while writing some of his famous short stories?

A. Weymouth, home of novelist James Boyd.

———◆———

Q. What Charlotte art center houses a large poster gallery?

A. Queens Gallery and Art Center.

———◆———

Q. Renowned writer David Stick has concentrated all of his efforts on what region of the state?

A. The coastal area.

———◆———

Q. Who organized the North Carolina Symphony Orchestra?

A. Dr. Benjamin Swalin.

———◆———

Q. What North Carolina author made history by becoming the first woman in the state to file as a candidate for governor?

A. Nancy Roberts.

Q. Who penned the words to the North Carolina state song?

A. William Gaston.

———◆———

Q. What two newspapers won Pulitzer prizes in 1953 for their articles about the Ku Klux Klan?

A. *The Tabor City Tribune* and the Whiteville *News Reporter.*

———◆———

Q. What Raleigh area is considered one of the best examples of an unspoiled Victorian neighborhood in the United States?

A. Historic Oakwood.

———◆———

Q. James Street is most famous for what novel, published the same year he moved to North Carolina?

A. *The Gauntlet,* 1945.

———◆———

Q. What summer school for musicians was founded by James Christian Pfohl in 1936?

A. The Transylvania Music Camp.

———◆———

Q. The new facilities for the North Carolina Museum of Art in Raleigh opened in what year?

A. 1983.

———◆———

Q. What is the title of a book by George F. Scheer, written in the form of a diary of a young Revolutionary soldier?

A. *Yankee Doodle Boy.*

Q. What is the title of the last known dated Richard Champion Bristol porcelain piece on display at the Charlotte Mint Museum?

A. *Grief.*

Q. Chapel Hill professor emeritus Vermont Royster retired from editing what prestigious business newspaper?

A. *The Wall Street Journal.*

Q. What 1971 novel by Daphne Athas was listed by *Time* magazine as one of the year's ten best works of fiction?

A. *Entering Ephesus.*

Q. Ben Haas authored what novel depicting the unsolved murder of a girl in Manteo?

A. *Daisy Canfield,* 1973.

Q. What North Carolina author released *The Cheerleader* and *July 7th* simultaneously in 1984?

A. Jill McCorkle.

Q. In what town is the annual Arts in the Park Festival held?

A. Laurinburg.

Q. North Carolina newspaperman John Harden authored what 1954 book containing thirty-three suspenseful ghost stories?

A. *Tar Heel Ghosts.*

Q. Who was the author who grew up in Boiling Springs and wrote the 1941 classic analysis and interpretation of the South entitled *The Mind of the South*?

A. W. J. Cash.

———◆———

Q. What Baden-born author wrote the humorous 1976 adolescent novel, *Confessions of a Champeen Fire Baton Twirler?*

A. Heather Ross Miller.

———◆———

Q. The first book written about North Carolina was published under what title?

A. *A briefe and true report of the new found land of Virginia.*

———◆———

Q. What newspaperman wrote three biographies for young readers: *Stonewall Jackson,* 1959; *Mosby, Gray Ghost of the Confederacy,* 1959; and *Robert E. Lee,* 1960?

A. Jonathan Daniels.

———◆———

Q. What is the oldest Catholic institution of higher learning in the southern Atlantic states?

A. Belmont Abbey College.

———◆———

Q. The 1975 North Carolina Award winner, Doris Betts, was born in what community?

A. Statesville.

———◆———

Q. What newspaper, begun in 1928, refers to itself as the world's smallest daily newspaper?

A. *The Tryon Daily Bulletin* (It is the size of a sheet of $8\frac{1}{2} \times 11$-inch typing paper).

Q. What member of the original 1585 colony of Roanoke Island created seventy-five famous paintings of the Indian life he observed?

A. John White.

———◆———

Q. What author of *Woodrow's Trumpet* was called a "Southern Nelson Algren"?

A. Tim McLaurin.

———◆———

Q. What ballad retold the story of a historic train wreck on July 27, 1911, in Richmond County?

A. "The Hamlet Wreck."

———◆———

Q. From what two counties did Bernice Kelly Harris glean background for seven novels?

A. Northampton and Wake counties.

———◆———

Q. The Annual American Indian Dance Festival may be enjoyed in what city?

A. Wilmington.

———◆———

Q. Author Phillips Russell was born in what community?

A. Rockingham.

———◆———

Q. What artist, whose works are now seen at the Metropolitan Museum of Art and the National Gallery, lived in Fayetteville as a child?

A. Elliott Daingerfield.

Q. What phrase did Stephen Foster originally use for the first line of "Old Folks at Home"?

A. "Way Down Upon the Pee Dee River."

———◆———

Q. Longtime-resident of Chapel Hill, Betty Smith, wrote what novel said to be one of the ten best-selling books of all time?

A. *A Tree Grows in Brooklyn,* 1943.

———◆———

Q. Where in 1897 was the first tax-supported library established in North Carolina?

A. Durham.

———◆———

Q. What 1960 book by Burke Davis gives much information not previously published about our battling ancestors?

A. *Our Incredible Civil War.*

———◆———

Q. Durham native Sylvia Wilkinson wrote *The Stainless Steel Carrot,* 1971, borrowing from her love and enthusiasm for what sport?

A. Sports car racing.

———◆———

Q. Who produced the sculpture entitled *Women of the Confederacy* for the Capitol Square in Raleigh?

A. Augustus Lukman.

———◆———

Q. In the 1840s and 1850s, what Wilmington minister received acclaim for his stage portrayals of women?

A. The Rt. Rev. William Mercer Green.

Q. What annual art show is held at Salisbury?

A. The North Carolina Artists Invitational.

———◆———

Q. What famous slave poet sold his poems to university students at Chapel Hill for twenty-five to seventy-five cents, which they in turn sent to their sweethearts?

A. George Moses Horton.

———◆———

Q. In 1937 LeGette Blythe wrote the biography of what general who once had served under Napoleon?

A. Marshall Ney.

———◆———

Q. What author is known as the first native Tar Heel to write a book for children?

A. Mary Ann Mason, *A Wreath from the Woods of Carolina*, 1859.

———◆———

Q. In what community was Hobson Pittman, a well-known twentieth-century painter, born?

A. Tarboro.

———◆———

Q. What book was the first published work written by a Negro in the South?

A. *The Hope of Liberty*.

———◆———

Q. What author was the first minister of the Village Chapel in Pinehurst?

A. Edward Everett Hale.

Q. What honor was bestowed upon Vermont Royster by President Ronald Reagan on May 12, 1986?

A. The Presidential Medal of Freedom for his service in journalism and communications.

———◆———

Q. John Ehle wrote what novel in 1967 describing the hardships of building a railroad from Old Fort to Ridgecrest?

A. *The Road.*

———◆———

Q. What newspaperman born in Mecklenburg County authored a series of New Testament biblical novels beginning with *Bold Galilean*, 1948?

A. LeGette Blythe.

———◆———

Q. What Berea-born poet served as the secretary of the North Carolina State Department of Art, Culture, and History?

A. Sam Ragan.

———◆———

Q. What Raleigh-born author compiled the first collection of North Carolina poetry, *Wood-notes; or Carolina Carols?*

A. Mary Bayard Clarke, pen name, *Tenella.*

———◆———

Q. What North Carolina native and dancer with the New York City Ballet won the first Carolina Prize for outstanding work in the visual or performing arts?

A. Mel Tomlinson.

———◆———

Q. A World War II juvenile mystery written by Nell Wise Wechter and set on Cape Hatteras was published under what title?

A. *Taffy of Torpedo Junction,* 1957.

Q. What film, based on *The Clansman* by Thomas Dixon, Jr., became the first epic in movie history?

A. *The Birth of a Nation.*

———◆———

Q. What North Carolinian penned the comedy "Blackbeard," which played in New York's Bowery Theater in 1833?

A. Lemuel Sawyer.

———◆———

Q. "The Tree Carver," R. K. Harniman, sculpted what he calls "the world's largest wooden sculpture," which stands in Manteo, using what tool?

A. A chain saw.

———◆———

Q. Known for her poetry and short stories, Olive Tilford Dargan wrote three novels, *Call Home the Heart,* 1932; *A Stone Came Rolling,* 1935; and *Sons of the Stranger,* 1947, using what pseudonym?

A. Fielding Burke.

———◆———

Q. What Tom Wicker novel is based on a famous senatorial campaign in North Carolina?

A. *The Kingpin,* 1953.

———◆———

Q. What was the last novel written by Thomas Dixon, Jr.?

A. *The Flaming Sword,* 1939.

———◆———

Q. Award winning poet A. R. Ammons was born in what county?

A. Columbus.

Q. What North Carolina journalist authored *Where's Mark Twain When We Really Need Him?*

A. Jerry Bledsoe.

◆

Q. What Chapel Hill author/historian wrote *First Steps in North Carolina History?*

A. Cornelia Phillips Spencer.

◆

Q. Guy Owen, born near Clarkton, authored what humorous novel based on the Cape Fear River basin?

A. *The Ballad of the Flim-Flam Man.*

◆

Q. What outstanding painter headed the Permanent Art School at Blowing Rock?

A. Elliot Daingerfield.

◆

Q. What historical novelist wrote of Colonial and Revolutionary times in and around Albemarle?

A. Inglis Fletcher.

◆

Q. Where is the Snuffy Jenkins Music Park?

A. Cliffside.

◆

Q. What primitive sculptor carved the history of North Carolina on a 7,000-pound mottled green nephrite jade boulder?

A. Richard Sipe.

Q. What Winston-Salem facility for exhibiting modern art and sculpture was once the residence of James G. Hanes, founder of Hanes Hosiery, Inc.?

A. Southeastern Center of Contemporary Art.

———◆———

Q. What eastern North Carolina historian born in Bladen County wrote *Stories of the Old Cherokees?*

A. F. Roy Johnson.

———◆———

Q. What book was the first novel about North Carolina people to win a literary award?

A. *Purslane,* by Bernice Kelly Harris, 1939.

———◆———

Q. Suzanne Newton, born in Bunnlevel, wrote of her brother's cat in a children's book by what title?

A. *Purro and the Prattleberries.*

———◆———

Q. What novel by Robert Ruark unfolds the story of a North Carolina boy who becomes a ruthless business tycoon?

A. *Poor No More,* 1959.

———◆———

Q. Ovid Williams Pierce, author of *The Plantation,* 1953, and *On a Lonesome Porch,* 1960, was born in what northeastern North Carolina community?

A. Weldon.

———◆———

Q. What writers' organization, started in 1984, has more than 1200 members?

A. The North Carolina Writers Network.

SPORTS & LEISURE

CHAPTER FIVE

Q. What two Williamston-born brothers are the only brothers ever to have received baseball's Cy Young Award?

A. Jim and Gaylord Perry.

———◆———

Q. Where may you see Dwight D. Eisenhower's golf cart displayed?

A. The World Golf Hall of Fame, Pinehurst.

———◆———

Q. What seventy-seven-acre theme park is built in two states, North Carolina and South Carolina?

A. Carowinds.

———◆———

Q. Professional basketball player Meadowlark Lemon was born in what city?

A. Wilmington.

———◆———

Q. Which jersey number was worn by legendary Charlie ("Choo Choo") Justice?

A. Number 22.

Q. What North Carolina resident is a top money winner and one of the most famous stock-car racers of all time?

A. Richard Petty.

———◆———

Q. The Shad Festival, a five-day event held in early April, is celebrated in what community?

A. Grifton.

———◆———

Q. What Lowell-born major league first baseman continued his career by taking over management of the Chicago Cubs from Leo Durocher in 1972?

A. Carroll Walter ("Whitey") Lockman.

———◆———

Q. By what name are seafood restaurants in North Carolina sometimes called?

A. Seafood Camps.

———◆———

Q. In 1982 the Pinehurst Hotel and Country Club installed four areas of courts for what ancient sport?

A. Croquet.

———◆———

Q. Statesville is host to what annual aeronautical event?

A. America's oldest Hot Air Balloon Rally.

———◆———

Q. What former basketball player, now a sportscaster, was inducted into the Wake Forest University Hall of Fame in 1977?

A. Billy Packer.

Q. What Wake Forest University alumnus has captured the Masters Golf Tournament four times?

A. Arnold Palmer.

———◆———

Q. The gathering of Scottish clans held in Red Springs the first weekend in October includes what special event?

A. The Flora MacDonald Highland Games.

———◆———

Q. What Stokes County lifeguard taught many children to swim and began the Roger Dodger Club for his students?

A. Pompey ("Mac Pete") Cardwell.

———◆———

Q. What Ocracoke inn was used as a public school until the 1930s?

A. Island Inn.

———◆———

Q. What town holds an annual ramps festival?

A. Waynesville.

———◆———

Q. What is the mascot of North Carolina State?

A. A wolf.

———◆———

Q. The twenty-sixth Annual Masters Water Ski Tournament Championship (1985) went to what Greenville native in the category of Women's Tricks?

A. Kristi Overton.

Q. What was the nickname of the 1890 Durham-born World Series veteran, George Whitted?

A. "Possum."

Q. Where is the world's only gourd museum?

A. Fuquay-Varina, Wake County.

Q. Where is the U.S. Open King Mackerel Tournament held?

A. Southport.

Q. Approximately how many miles of bicycling highways have been selected and mapped through the office of the Bicycle Program of the North Carolina Department of Transportation?

A. 1,500.

Q. Which North Carolina basketball star played for Denver from 1975 to 1978 and was traded to the Philadelphia 76ers in 1979?

A. Bobby Jones.

Q. When the new fitness trail was opened at Lake Marion, what was cut instead of a ribbon?

A. Shoelaces.

Q. In what bowl game did North Carolina shut out Air Force 35–0?

A. Gator Bowl, 1963.

Q. The 1938 Duke University basketball team earned what nickname?

A. "Never a Dull Moment Boys."

Q. What three-day competition is held annually at America's highest sand dune on the Outer Banks?

A. The Hang Gliding Spectacular.

Q. Charlotte Motor Speedway hosts what NASCAR-approved, late-model stock car race in May?

A. The World 600.

Q. Jim Bibby, major league pitcher from Franklinton, played for what four clubs during his ten-year career?

A. St. Louis Cardinals, Texas Rangers, Cleveland Indians, and Pittsburgh Pirates.

Q. What event in which sailors compete in homemade vessels is held annually at New Bern?

A. The Great Trent River Raft Race.

Q. The North Carolina Maritime Museum is in what town?

A. Beaufort.

Q. American-made clocks of all types and sizes are available for viewing at what North Carolina museum?

A. The Greensboro Clock Museum.

Q. What 100-mile international bicycle race originated in Southern Pines in 1976?

A. Tour de Moore.

◆

Q. The Triad Tennis Tournament is held in what city?

A. Greensboro.

◆

Q. Burton Edwards of Maggie Valley won what world championship in 1981 at the age of eighteen?

A. World Champion Clogger.

◆

Q. What type of record fish was caught in 1972 by James M. Hussey on Hatteras Inlet?

A. Bluefish, 31 pounds, 12 ounces.

◆

Q. What two North Carolina brothers formed the Ferrell battery for the Boston Red Sox and Washington Senators for nearly five years?

A. Richard Benjamin ("Rick") Ferrell and Wesley Cheek ("Wes") Ferrell.

◆

Q. In 1958 what county organized a wagon train that makes a journey each year and finishes with a parade through a selected mountain community on the Fourth of July?

A. Cherokee.

◆

Q. In what year did Richard Petty begin competing in NAS-CAR races?

A. 1958.

Q. In what city is the Schiele Museum of Natural History and Planetarium which features a ten-building Pioneer Site and a Catawba Indian Village?

A. Gastonia.

———◆———

Q. Gil Coan, who played eleven years for the Washington Senators, Baltimore Orioles, Chicago White Sox, and New York Giants was born in what community?

A. Monroe.

———◆———

Q. What eleven-hundred-acre park featuring riding, swimming, golf, and camping was formerly the lavish estate of William and Kate B. Reynolds?

A. Tanglewood Park, Clemmons.

———◆———

Q. What Maggie Valley resident became known as the "grandfather of clogging" during the 1920s?

A. Sam Queen.

———◆———

Q. Wake Forest football star Brian Piccolo played five seasons for which pro team?

A. Chicago Bears, 1965–1969.

———◆———

Q. With what team did Meadowlark Lemon play from 1954 to 1978?

A. The Harlem Globetrotters.

———◆———

Q. What Winston-Salem–born Army veteran bowled an average of 193 during his sixteen years with the ABC tournaments and was inducted into the American Bowling Congress Hall of Fame?

A. Ed Easter.

Q. What Caroleen-born major league catcher was better known for his pinch-hitting with a batting average of .295?

A. Forrest Harrill ("Smoky") Burgess.

———◆———

Q. A three-day Spot Festival is held every October in what community?

A. Hampstead.

———◆———

Q. What general's complaint that Charlotte was "a hornet's nest" led to the current name of the city's NBA franchise?

A. Lord Cornwallis.

———◆———

Q. The U.S. Nationals are hosted each September by what Richmond County dragway?

A. The Rockingham International Dragway.

———◆———

Q. What museum features a thirty-seven-bay roundhouse and presents the history of transportation in North Carolina?

A. Spencer Shops State Historic Site.

———◆———

Q. What type of automobile display can be seen about one mile west of Mill Spring in Polk County?

A. Willard Jolley's Edsel Collection.

———◆———

Q. Tom Alexander opened the first southern ski resort in what North Carolina county?

A. Haywood.

Q. Which World Series pitcher, born in 1894 at Oxford, played for the St. Louis Cardinals, Philadelphia Phillies, and Pittsburgh Pirates and was the first major league moundsman to wear glasses during play?

A. Henry Lee ("Specs") Meadows.

✦

Q. What unusual type of community is found in Brunswick County, the only one of its kind in North Carolina?

A. A nudist colony.

✦

Q. Hillsborough is the home of what museum featuring over 100 musical devices?

A. Doyle Lane's Music Box Museum.

✦

Q. What Hendersonville native played end for the Washington Redskins through 1964 and for Green Bay in 1965 before retiring after the 1966 season?

A. Walter W. Anderson.

✦

Q. What popular pastime calls for the use of a single string and a long-handled net?

A. Crabbing.

✦

Q. What former Pittsburgh Steelers team captain became the first black sheriff in North Carolina?

A. John Baker.

✦

Q. What was the first professional tour title won by Arnold Palmer?

A. The Canadian Open, 1955.

Q. What transportation museum, located in Cherryville, is the only one of its kind in the nation?

A. The Trucking Museum, owned by Grier Beam.

———◆———

Q. Grandfather Mountain provides the setting for what sporting event, open only to experts in the sport?

A. The Masters of Hang Gliding Championship.

———◆———

Q. Who accepted the head football coaching position at Wake Forest in March, 1981?

A. Al Groh.

———◆———

Q. Fayetteville-born Cal Koonce pitched a total of ten years for what three major league clubs?

A. Chicago Cubs, New York Giants, and Boston Red Sox.

———◆———

Q. What former University of North Carolina quarterback created the original Putt Putt Miniature Golf Course?

A. Don Clayton.

———◆———

Q. Born in Stanley, March 6, 1933, what major league baseball player pitched fourteen years and was known for his unique style of underhand pitching?

A. Ted Wade Abernathy.

———◆———

Q. The Mountain Marathon, second only to the Pikes Peak Marathon in difficulty, is an event run between which two mountains?

A. Boone and Grandfather mountains.

Q. What Concord-born infielder became the American League's batting champion in 1950 with a .354 average in 110 games for Boston?

A. William Dale ("Billy") Goodman.

———◆———

Q. As of 1990, how many times has Coach Dean Smith led the University of North Carolina basketball team to the NCAA "Final Four"?

A. Seven.

———◆———

Q. What wealthy planter from near Graysburg was the last owner of the famous racehorse sire, Sir Archy?

A. William D. Amis.

———◆———

Q. William Fuller of the University of North Carolina played for which two USFL teams?

A. Philadelphia and Baltimore.

———◆———

Q. What Duke basketball player holds the career individual record for most points scored?

A. Mike Gminski, 1977–1980.

———◆———

Q. Carolina athlete David Drechsler joined what pro team in 1983?

A. Green Bay Packers.

———◆———

Q. What was the original school mascot of Wake Forest?

A. The tiger.

Q. What North Carolina-born pitcher hit a home run his first time at bat in the majors and never hit another in his twenty-one-year career?

A. James H. ("Hoyt") Wilhelm.

Q. The biggest steam engine show in the South is a Fourth of July weekend event in what town?

A. Denton.

Q. How many hubcaps are on display at the Hubcap King Museum, Madison?

A. Over 3,000.

Q. What nickname stuck with Wake Forest University in 1922?

A. The Demon Deacons.

Q. The University of North Carolina is credited with what "first" play during a football game with Georgia in Atlanta on October 26, 1895?

A. The first forward pass.

Q. What University of North Carolina swimmer won eleven national championships and set three U.S. records?

A. Sue Walsh.

Q. The residents of Union County, North Carolina, and Lancaster County, South Carolina, promote a football game annually using top athletes from area high schools to decide the birthplace of which historical figure?

A. Andrew Jackson.

Q. New Bern hosts what sporting event in mid-February for amateurs from the East Coast?

A. Racquetball Tournament of Champions.

———◆———

Q. North Carolina State University is known by what nickname?

A. Wolfpack.

———◆———

Q. What museum displays President Dwight D. Eisenhower's $250,000 armored limousine, a 1930 sixteen-cylinder Cadillac used in several Humphrey Bogart movies, and other unique cars from the Jim Nelson collection?

A. Tryon Antique Car Museum.

———◆———

Q. New Bern was the birthplace of what famous soft drink?

A. Pepsi Cola.

———◆———

Q. Born in Laurinburg, Wes Covington played what position during his eleven-year career in the major leagues?

A. Outfielder.

———◆———

Q. In 1981 North Carolina defeated Arkansas, 31–27, in what bowl game?

A. Gator Bowl, Jacksonville.

———◆———

Q. What Charlotte radio station is the oldest in North Carolina?

A. WBT, first broadcast in 1922.

Q. Reidsville hosts what competitive contest on the second weekend of November?

A. The North Carolina–Virginia Horseshoeing Association Contest, the second largest in the nation.

◆

Q. What convention honoring one of America's top sportsmen is held annually at Level Cross?

A. The Richard Petty Fan Club Convention.

◆

Q. With nineteen varsity and ten junior varsity sports, what high school has the largest all-around athletic program in the state?

A. Chapel Hill High School.

◆

Q. Pep Young, born in Jamestown, played infield for what three National League ball clubs?

A. Pittsburgh Pirates, Cincinnati Reds, and St. Louis Cardinals.

◆

Q. Where is the National Whistling Convention held in April each year?

A. Louisburg.

◆

Q. What race track is home to the Mello Yellow 300?

A. Charlotte Motor Speedway.

◆

Q. What Asheville resident won the Miss America crown in 1962?

A. Maria Fletcher.

Q. What North Carolina resident invented the hang glider?

A. Francis Rogallo.

———◆———

Q. Don Cardwell of Winston-Salem pitched for which five National League clubs?

A. Philadelphia Phillies, Chicago Cubs, Pittsburgh Pirates, New York Giants, and Atlanta Braves.

———◆———

Q. The 82nd Airborne Division conducts training sessions in what activity that can be viewed by the general public?

A. Parachuting.

———◆———

Q. Who is the only ball player in National League history to hit two grand slam homeruns in one game?

A. Pitcher, Tony Cloninger.

———◆———

Q. The University of North Carolina, Charlotte, is a member of what conference?

A. Sun Belt.

———◆———

Q. What High Point-born major league Hall of Famer was voted greatest White Sox player of all time?

A. Lucius Benjamin ("Luke") Appling.

———◆———

Q. The Ava Gardner Museum, featuring memorabilia and movies from her Hollywood days, is found in what county?

A. Johnston County (Smithfield).

Q. Who in 1941 became the original student Deacon at Wake Forest?

A. Jack Baldwin.

———◆———

Q. The jerseys of which five football greats have been retired at the University of North Carolina?

A. Charlie ("Choo Choo") Justice, Cotton Sutherland, Art Weiner, Andy Bershak, and George Barclay.

———◆———

Q. What former North Carolina alumnus played in the NBA for Washington from 1977 to 1981 and then was traded to the Los Angeles Lakers in 1982?

A. Mitch Kupchak.

———◆———

Q. Where is the International Volks march held each September?

A. Winston-Salem.

———◆———

Q. Wake Forest is a member of what conference?

A. Atlantic Coast.

———◆———

Q. What sporting event that dates back to pre-Columbian times takes place the second weekend in October at Cherokee?

A. A stick ball game.

———◆———

Q. What town is the home of the annual Dog Days Sailing Regatta?

A. Aurora.

Q. What Scottish gathering in North Carolina is listed as the finest of its kind in this country?

A. The Grandfather Mountain Highland Games and Gathering of the Clans.

———◆———

Q. The running of the Northwestern Bank 400 Grand National Stock Car Race is held in what town?

A. North Wilkesboro.

———◆———

Q. Where is the North Carolina State Championship Charity Horse Show held?

A. Raleigh.

———◆———

Q. What New Hanover High School coach guided fifty-five football, basketball, and baseball teams to championships?

A. Leon Brogden.

———◆———

Q. Who coached the North Carolina Tar Heels' basketball team from 1945 to 1952?

A. Carl Snavely.

———◆———

Q. Durham is home for what minor league baseball franchise?

A. Durham Bulls.

———◆———

Q. Where is the Great Cardboard Box Derby held to celebrate the coming of cold weather?

A. Beech Mountain Resort.

Q. Born in Winston-Salem, what defensive end was drafted on the first round by the Minnesota Vikings and was a regular from 1964 to 1973?

A. Carl ("Moose") Eller.

———◆———

Q. What were the combined 1985 golf winnings of the Wake Forest Deacons?

A. $1,503,992.

———◆———

Q. High Point-born Ray Hayworth played fifteen years for the Detroit Tigers, Brooklyn Dodgers, New York Giants, and St. Louis Browns at what position?

A. Catcher.

———◆———

Q. The annual Sugar Cup Slalom is hosted by what resort?

A. Sugar Mountain, Banner Elk.

———◆———

Q. At what Cabarrus County attraction can visitors take a two-mile stagecoach ride and pet Himalayan bear cubs?

A. Buffalo Ranch.

———◆———

Q. Where is blowgun and bow and arrow competition held each year during Ramp Day festivities?

A. Cherokee.

———◆———

Q. Outstanding pitcher Catfish Hunter was born in what community?

A. Hertford.

Q. What charitable golf tournament is held at Bermuda Run Country Club in Winston-Salem?

A. The Bing Crosby National Championship.

———◆———

Q. Charlotte hosts what fifty-year-old sporting event in which North Carolina and South Carolina high school football stars compete against each other?

A. Shrine Bowl Game.

———◆———

Q. What North Carolina State basketball coach started the tradition of cutting down the net after a championship?

A. Everett N. Case.

———◆———

Q. What Carolina-bred All-Star moved to a coaching position with Denver in 1981?

A. Doug Moe.

———◆———

Q. Catfish Hunter pitched in how many World Series games?

A. Six: 1972, 1973, and 1974 with the Oakland A's, and 1976, 1977, and 1978 with the New York Yankees.

———◆———

Q. Robert Lindley of Snow Camp has a collection of what type of cars that were not produced after 1966?

A. Studebakers.

———◆———

Q. What Lexington-born second baseman invented the smooth double-play combination at Cincinnati with Ray McMillan and Ted Kluszewski?

A. John E. ("Johnny") Temple.

Q. ABC's "Monday Night Football" and "Monday Night Baseball" ex-commentator Howard Cosell was born in what city?

A. Winston-Salem.

Q. What is the oldest Masonic Lodge in North Carolina?

A. Saint John's Lodge (*circa* 1804).

Q. Who was the great Rocky Mount-born first baseman called the "Lou Gehrig of the Colored Leagues"?

A. Walter Fenner ("Buck") Leonard.

Q. The Swiss Bear Festival is celebrated annually in what community?

A. New Bern, Craven County.

Q. In what area is the North Carolina Oyster Festival held?

A. The South Brunswick Islands.

Q. Charlotte's annual SpringFest features what unusual racing event in which six people are tied together from start to finish?

A. The Southeastern Centipede Championship Race.

Q. What museum houses the Van Sant Armor Collection, featuring entire suits of armor, shields, and weapons?

A. The Asheville Art Museum.

Q. Born in Roxboro, what St. Louis Cardinal outfielder scored the winning run in the seventh game of the 1946 World Series against the Boston Red Sox?

A. Enos B. Slaughter.

———◆———

Q. What tournament is the largest of its kind in the South and is held the last weekend in July at the Winston-Salem Hilton?

A. The Lawrence G. Pfefferkorn Chess Tournament.

———◆———

Q. At what Beaufort event might you tempt your taste buds with such delicacies as marinated octopus, raw squid, or live sea urchin eggs?

A. The Hampton Mariners Museum's annual Strange Seafood Exhibit.

———◆———

Q. Where was pitching veteran Tony Cloninger born?

A. Lincoln.

———◆———

Q. Ayden in Pitt County hosts what annual event?

A. The Collard Festival.

———◆———

Q. Alvin Floyd ("General") Crowder, born in Winston-Salem, pitched sixteen straight victories while playing for what American League team?

A. Washington Senators.

———◆———

Q. What contest featuring a mountain toy is held in Osteen, just north of Asheville, the third Saturday of May?

A. The World Whimmy Diddle Contest.

Q. What community houses the National Railroad Museum and Hall of Fame?

A. Hamlet.

Q. What major league catcher, born in Lenoir, managed in the minor leagues, 1959–1964; coached with the Los Angeles Dodgers in 1958; coached the Washington Senators, 1965–1967; and coached the New York Mets, 1968–1972?

A. Albert B. ("Rube") Walker.

Q. Where was moundsman Johnny Lanning, who played for the Boston Braves and Pittsburgh Pirates, born?

A. Asheville.

Q. Who became the University of North Carolina's first All-American in 1934?

A. George Barclay.

Q. In what county is the National Whistlers Convention held?

A. Franklin.

Q. What is the name of the football stadium at North Carolina State?

A. Carter-Finley Stadium.

Q. What North Carolina resident is the proud father and promoter of "Bald-Headed Men of America" headquarters and convention?

A. John Capps.

Q. What dynamic North Carolina forward is the only player to be listed among the school's top ten in scoring, rebounding, and assists?

A. Mike O'Koren.

———◆———

Q. What is Howard Cosell's real name?

A. Howard Cohen.

———◆———

Q. Tanglewood Park, Clemmons, hosts what sporting event each spring?

A. The Tanglewood Steeplechase.

———◆———

Q. Mike Caldwell, who pitched a total of eleven years for the San Diego Padres, San Francisco Giants, Cincinnati Reds, and Milwaukee Brewers, is from what North Carolina town?

A. Tarboro.

———◆———

Q. What city holds the Oak Hollow Drag Boat Races, in which the world record speed was set at 215.82 m.p.h. in 1982 by Eddie Hill?

A. High Point.

———◆———

Q. Stock-car racing grew out of what activity common in the South?

A. Running moonshine.

———◆———

Q. What major league baseball player hit his first home run as a professional during spring training at Cape Fear Fairgrounds, Fayetteville?

A. Babe Ruth, 1914, with Baltimore Orioles.

Q. MacRae Meadows on Grandfather Mountain is the location for what ingathering of gospel music lovers?

A. Singing on the Mountain.

———◆———

Q. The stables at the Biltmore mansion are now used for what purpose?

A. As a restaurant.

———◆———

Q. Where is the 10,000 meter Leader Run in the Park held each year?

A. Raleigh.

———◆———

Q. Which third baseman, born in Mebane, played ten years for the St. Louis Cardinals, Cincinnati Reds, and Brooklyn Dodgers?

A. Lew Riggs.

———◆———

Q. What North Carolina community hosted the first million dollar bingo game?

A. Cherokee, 1983.

———◆———

Q. Charlie Yelton of Forest City constructed a house using what unusual building material?

A. Bottles, 11,987 of them.

———◆———

Q. The University of North Carolina won NCAA National Championships in basketball in what two years?

A. 1957 and 1982.

Q. The newest golf course at Pinehurst, Course No. 7, was designed by what architect?

A. Rees Jones.

———◆———

Q. Born in Rocky Mount, what infielder and outfielder played a total of eleven years for the Washington Senators, Cleveland Indians, and California Angels?

A. Chuck Hinton.

———◆———

Q. What North Carolina team won the Amateur Softball Association's Men's Major Slow Pitch National Championship in 1985?

A. Blanton's, Fayetteville.

———◆———

Q. The Tournament of Kings is the biggest-moneyed event in what type of competition?

A. Logging, $10,000 in prizes, plus expense-paid trips to the event.

———◆———

Q. What Wake Forest athlete was chosen in the first round by Washington in the 1985 NBA player draft?

A. Kenny Green.

———◆———

Q. Who became the first Duke University athlete to have his number retired?

A. Basketball great, Dick Groat, Number 10.

———◆———

Q. What ACC competitor seeks to kidnap the North Carolina mascot before the big game each year?

A. The Blue Devils of Duke.

Q. Who was the first black basketball player for the University of North Carolina?

A. Charlie Smith.

———◆———

Q. What Wilmington winery is well-known for its scuppernong dessert wine?

A. Duplin Wine Cellars.

———◆———

Q. Bob Stinson, catcher for the Los Angeles Dodgers, St. Louis Cardinals, Houston Astros, Montreal Expos, Kansas City Athletics, and Seattle Mariners, was born in what North Carolina community?

A. Elkin.

———◆———

Q. What museum displays a replica of the drugstore O. Henry worked in as a youth?

A. The Greensboro Historical Museum.

———◆———

Q. Charlotte-born Tommy Helms played infield for what four major league clubs?

A. Cincinnati Reds, Houston Astros, Pittsburgh Pirates, and Boston Red Sox.

———◆———

Q. What North Carolina golf club boasts the longest golf hole in the world?

A. Black Mountain Golf Club (the seventeenth, 745 yards, par 6).

———◆———

Q. The Greensboro's Mayor's Cup Sailing Regatta is held on what lake?

A. Lake Townsend.

Q. What Durham-born major league pitcher had his most successful years with the Los Angeles Dodgers and made his first of four appearances in the World Series with Brooklyn in 1955?

A. Roger Lee Craig.

Q. Burlington is home to what aerial race?

A. The Central Tar Heel Balloon Race.

Q. What noted spring horse race is held at Tryon?

A. The Block House Steeplechase.

Q. What North Carolina coach led the 1976 United States Olympic basketball team to a Gold Medal in Montreal?

A. Coach Dean Smith.

Q. At the 1984 Los Angeles Summer Olympic Games, which two North Carolina basketball stars were named co-captains of the winning United States team?

A. Michael Jordan and Sam Perkins.

Q. What arena is home court for North Carolina State?

A. Reynolds Coliseum.

Q. What annual stock car race is held in Wilkes County?

A. The Wilkes 400 Grand National Stock Car Race.

Q. What star pitcher, born in Greensboro, ended his career with a lifetime record of thirty-eight home runs, making him one of the greatest hitting pitchers in the majors?

A. Wesley Cheek ("Wes") Ferrell.

————◆————

Q. A grape stomp contest is held annually at what North Carolina winery?

A. Duplin Wine Cellars in Rose Hill.

————◆————

Q. What Huntsville-born major league Hall of Famer is known as the greatest relief pitcher of all time?

A. James H. ("Hoyt") Wilhelm.

————◆————

Q. At what speedway is the annual Unocal 76 Pit Crew Championship held?

A. North Carolina Speedway, Rockingham.

————◆————

Q. What tackle of Duke University was the first North Carolinian to be honored as an All-American by the national press associations and *Collier's* magazine?

A. Fred E. ("Freddie") Crawford.

————◆————

Q. Born in North Carolina, 1872, who was one of the first managers in the history of baseball to conduct meetings before and after the games to talk over strategy?

A. C. I. Taylor.

————◆————

Q. What unique wrestling event may be seen in Cherokee?

A. Bear wrestling.

Q. What left-handed pitcher, born in Clinton, played for the Cincinnati Reds and the New York Giants and during his career had a controversy arise over whether he had knowledge of a 1919 World Series game being fixed?

A. John C. ("Rube") Benton.

Q. What Richmond County resort was founded after a deer hunter discovered the local springs cleared up his hay-fever?

A. Ellerbe Springs Inn.

Q. What North Carolinian was named USFL Player of the Year in the league's first season?

A. Kelvin Bryant.

Q. In what museum does an exhibit display ladies' apparel from 1850 to 1940?

A. High Point Museum and Historical Park.

Q. What is the length of the Cape Hatteras Lighthouse Run?

A. Ten kilometers.

Q. What 1973 North Carolina graduate played professional basketball and received the head coaching position for the NBA Cleveland Cavaliers in 1985?

A. George Karl.

Q. What Tar Heel was named National Player of the Year in 1978?

A. Phil Ford.

Q. What Lenoir native pitched a total of thirteen years for the New York Yankees, Cleveland Indians, St. Louis Browns, Brooklyn Dodgers, and New York Giants with a lifetime record of 142 wins—75 losses?

A. Johnny Thomas Allen.

━━━━━◆━━━━━

Q. Where is the Flounder Jubilee Invitational Golf Tournament played?

A. New Bern.

━━━━━◆━━━━━

Q. What North Carolina State halfback played for the AFL Pittsburgh Steelers, Boston Patriots, New York Titans, and the New York Jets?

A. Richard Christy.

━━━━━◆━━━━━

Q. Which university captured the NCAA Golf championship in 1986?

A. Wake Forest.

━━━━━◆━━━━━

Q. What game of ball was brought from Italy to the Blue Ridge Mountains by the Waldenses?

A. Bocci.

━━━━━◆━━━━━

Q. The Tuckaseigee Classic held at Sylva is what type of sporting event?

A. Men's softball tournament.

━━━━━◆━━━━━

Q. What nickname was given to the University of North Carolina's 1922 star quarterback, Jack Merritt?

A. "The Battering Ram."

Q. What type of schooling can be found at the community of Beaufort, the first of its kind in the world?

A. A pirate's school.

———◆———

Q. Victor G. Sorrell of Morrisville, who coached baseball at North Carolina State University, 1945–1966, pitched ten years for what major league club?

A. Detroit Tigers.

———◆———

Q. Near what town is Sliding Rock, a 150-foot natural water slide?

A. Brevard.

———◆———

Q. What is the name of the University of North Carolina's mascot?

A. Rameses.

———◆———

Q. What North Carolina basketball player achieved overseas success by winning European Player of the Year three times?

A. Doug Moe.

———◆———

Q. In what unusual sporting event held annually at Morehead City do all the losers become supper?

A. The Blue Crab Derby.

———◆———

Q. Where are the Southeastern Brittany Field Trials held?

A. Hoffman.

Q. What former North Carolina athlete was named 1985 NBA Rookie of the Year with the Chicago Bulls?

A. Michael Jordan.

———◆———

Q. Born in Wilmington, who became the eleventh quarterback in NFL history to gain more than 25,000 yards passing?

A. Roman ("Gabe") Gabriel.

———◆———

Q. What water race is held in June at Roanoke Rapids near Halifax?

A. The Great Roanoke River Raft Race.

———◆———

Q. Wilkes County is the location for what fall festival?

A. The Brushy Mountain Apple Festival.

———◆———

Q. What community is known as the "barbecue center of the universe"?

A. Lexington.

———◆———

Q. Which immortalized North Carolina football star played pro ball for the Washington Redskins in 1950, 1952–1954?

A. Charlie ("Choo Choo") Justice.

———◆———

Q. What fishing tournament is held each June at Atlantic Beach?

A. Cap'n Fannie's Billfish Tournament.

Q. What biking event is held on the Blue Ridge Parkway?

A. The Crest of the World Bike Race.

———◆———

Q. In the fall of 1973, which North Carolina basketball star helped the United States squad take the title at the World University Games in Moscow?

A. Mitch Kupchak.

———◆———

Q. What are Wake Forest's school colors?

A. Black and gold.

———◆———

Q. North Carolina quarterback Scott Stankavage signed with what pro team in 1984?

A. Denver.

———◆———

Q. What Winston-Salem establishment was originally a furnace room used as a part of the heating system for the R. J. Reynolds estate?

A. La Chaudiere.

———◆———

Q. Mid-August is the time of year for what annual water event held at Chimney Rock?

A. The Wash Tub Races.

———◆———

Q. Who was the University of North Carolina's athletic business manager who appropriated twenty-five dollars to purchase the school's first mascot?

A. Charlie Woollen.

Q. How many cigarettes does R. J. Reynolds Tobacco USA produce each day?

A. More than 450 million.

—◆—

Q. During which year did the University of North Carolina boast its first basketball team?

A. 1911.

—◆—

Q. In 1949 which University of North Carolina football player caught a record fifty-two passes?

A. Art Weiner.

—◆—

Q. What Graham-born pitcher was best known for giving up Babe Ruth's sixtieth home run in 1927?

A. Jonathan Thomas ("Tom") Zachary.

—◆—

Q. What team did the University of North Carolina play in the 1983 Peach Bowl?

A. Florida State.

—◆—

Q. In January, 1986 where was the Silver and Snow Carnival held, commemorating twenty-five years of skiing in North Carolina?

A. The Cataloochee Ski Area.

—◆—

Q. Where is the 10,000 meter Observer Marathon held?

A. Charlotte.

SCIENCE & NATURE

C H A P T E R   S I X

Q. North Carolina's fragile barrier islands are referred to by what name?

A. The Outer Banks.

———◆———

Q. What Chapel Hill chemist developed the process for turning southern pine trees into newsprint?

A. Charles Herty.

———◆———

Q. What is the official state tree?

A. Pine (*Pinus palustris*).

———◆———

Q. What continent was first opened to the public at the North Carolina Zoological Park?

A. Africa.

———◆———

Q. Where was a piece of the original wing covering of the Wright Brothers' Airplane placed in July, 1969?

A. On the moon by astronauts Edwin ("Buzz") Aldrin and Neil Armstrong.

Q. What mountain-grown evergreen is picked and used for floral decoration?

A. Galax.

———◆———

Q. What is the largest natural lake in North Carolina?

A. Lake Mattamuskeet, fifteen miles long and six miles wide.

———◆———

Q. North Carolina leads the nation in the growing and manufacturing of what agricultural product?

A. Tobacco.

———◆———

Q. Who planted the first successful commercial peach orchard in 1928 in the Candor area?

A. M. R. Clark.

———◆———

Q. What National Wildlife Refuge, situated midway in the Atlantic flyway, is noted for large flocks of migratory snow geese?

A. Pea Island.

———◆———

Q. Bailey, in Nash County, houses what medical museum that features early equipment and a medicinal garden?

A. The Country Doctor Museum.

———◆———

Q. Where may stalactites and stalagmites be seen along an underground river?

A. Linville Caverns.

Q. What is the name of America's highest sand dune found at Nags Head?

A. Jockey's Ridge.

———◆———

Q. Burgaw is known for producing what fruit?

A. Blueberries.

———◆———

Q. What Swain County geological feature did the Indians believe to be haunted?

A. Nantahala Gorge.

———◆———

Q. What is North Carolina's only cheese manufacturing plant?

A. Ashe County Cheese.

———◆———

Q. Listed as one of the nation's top ten science museums, which Charlotte exhibit hall encourages hands-on learning?

A. Discovery Place.

———◆———

Q. Who was the pharmacist who mixed the concoction resulting in the new soft drink Pepsi Cola?

A. Caleb ("Doc") Bradham.

———◆———

Q. What are the names of the three land regions in the state?

A. The Atlantic Coastal Plain, the Piedmont, and the Blue Ridge (or Mountain).

Q. What physician was responsible for lowering Wilmington's death rate from 29.4 per 1000 in 1911 to 16.4 per 1000 in 1915?

A. Dr. Charles Nesbitt.

Q. What is the largest man-made lake in North Carolina?

A. Lake Norman.

Q. How many national forests are in North Carolina?

A. Four: Croatan, Nantahala, Pisgah, and Uwharrie (The Cherokee National Forest is divided between North Carolina and Tennessee).

Q. What type of bear lives in the Great Smoky Mountains?

A. Black bear.

Q. Moore County is known for what type of fossil deposits?

A. Petrified wood.

Q. The Lakes Pocosin area derives its name from an Algonquin term meaning what?

A. "Swamp" or "dismal."

Q. What tree noted for its "knees" is common in swamp areas of the state?

A. Cypress.

Q. Chadbourn, in Columbus County, hosts the oldest fruit festival in the South, featuring what fruit?

A. Strawberries.

Q. How long are the Outer Banks?

A. 320 miles.

Q. Treeless, grassy prairies covering the eastern coastal plain are known by what name?

A. Savannas.

Q. What planetarium annually presents the "Star of Bethlehem" program that scientifically examines the star of the Magi?

A. Morehead Planetarium in Chapel Hill.

Q. How many acres of national forest are in North Carolina?

A. 1.2 million acres.

Q. Scott's Hill is the home of what plantation that was one of the state's first and biggest peanut plantations?

A. Poplars' Grove.

Q. At what fall activity at the North Carolina Marine Resources Center on Roanoke Island do participants seek out unusual, edible seafoods and wild plants?

A. The October Marsh and Sea Festival.

Q. What community was re-incorporated in 1952 to serve as the center for the Sandhills Game Management Area?

A. Hoffman.

———◆———

Q. What state forest has the "Talking Tree Trail"?

A. Holmes State Forest.

———◆———

Q. America's largest post oak, with a crown spread of ninety-two feet and a height of ninety-four feet, stands on the campus of what institution of higher learning?

A. The University of North Carolina.

———◆———

Q. What commodity was first planted commercially near Elizabeth City?

A. Soybeans.

———◆———

Q. The North Carolina Botanical Gardens, known as the largest of its kind in the Southeast, covers how many acres?

A. 330 acres.

———◆———

Q. The only operating gold mine in the Southeast is in what county?

A. Stanly.

———◆———

Q. What rare World War II seaplane sits atop the deck of the U.S.S. *North Carolina?*

A. A Vought Kingfisher.

Q. Duke University conducts scientific research amounting to how many dollars annually?

A. Approximately $50 million.

Q. How many pounds of rice were produced in North Carolina in 1860?

A. Eight million.

Q. Ti-Caro of Gastonia is known for selling billions of yards of red-orange thread, used for what purpose?

A. Sewing jeans.

Q. Who founded the Academy of Arts and Sciences, the first scientific school in North Carolina?

A. The Reverend James Hall, Presbyterian minister.

Q. Where in Asheville can you see woolen cloth made, from fleece to the finished product?

A. The Biltmore Homespun Shops.

Q. What convention, organized by George Fawcett of Lincolnton, is held every Father's Day weekend at the Science Nature Center in Winston-Salem?

A. The UFO Convention.

Q. The Pharmacy Museum, acclaimed by the Smithsonian Institution as one of the finest in America, is in what city?

A. Durham.

Q. What tobacco manufacturer began in North Carolina and became the largest in the world?

A. Duke's American Tobacco Company.

———◆———

Q. The North Carolina Museum of Life and Science is in which city?

A. Durham.

———◆———

Q. The area around Cameron and Vass is known for what type of fruit?

A. The dewberry.

———◆———

Q. What plant is the largest producer of cigarettes in North Carolina and the second largest in the world?

A. R. J. Reynold's Whitaker Park Plant, Winston-Salem.

———◆———

Q. Where is the nation's highest manned weather station?

A. Atop Grandfather Mountain.

———◆———

Q. The Powell-Trollinger kilns in Catawba County began producing what product about 1870?

A. Lime.

———◆———

Q. Edwin M. Holt, textile innovator, created the first factory-dyed cotton cloth in the South by what name?

A. Alamance plaid.

Q. Known as the largest of its kind in America, what tree standing south of the Woodville community is 120 feet high, with a crown spread of 126 feet?

A. The Cherrybark Oak.

———◆———

Q. What German doctor was brought to the Biltmore estate to manage the surrounding forest?

A. Carl A. Schenck.

———◆———

Q. The study of what data led the Wright Brothers to choose Kitty Hawk for their flight experiments?

A. National Weather Bureau reports.

———◆———

Q. The Mount Olive Pickle Company produces how many jars of pickles each year?

A. Twenty-five million.

———◆———

Q. Mattamuskeet National Wildlife Refuge is famous for what beautiful bird?

A. Whistling swan.

———◆———

Q. How many varieties of fungi have been collected in the Great Smoky Mountains National Park?

A. Approximately 2,000.

———◆———

Q. What are the four small state forests that lie within North Carolina?

A. Clemmons, Holmes, Rendezvous Mountain, and Tuttle.

Q. What festival is held in Avery County the third weekend in October to help predict the weather of the coming winter?

A. The Woolly Worm Festival.

———◆———

Q. Weymouth Estate in Southern Pines includes about 150 acres of what type of tree, the largest grove of its kind in America?

A. Virgin pines.

———◆———

Q. For what metal did Thomas Edison enlist William Earl Hidden to prospect in Alexander County in 1879?

A. Platinum.

———◆———

Q. What is the "hands-on" science museum in Wilson?

A. Imagination Station.

———◆———

Q. On what grounds is the nation's largest azalea garden?

A. The Biltmore mansion.

———◆———

Q. The Aurora Fossil Museum displays fossils found during mining operations of what mineral?

A. Phosphate.

———◆———

Q. What national park on the North Carolina–Tennessee border is the most visited in the United States each year?

A. The Great Smoky Mountains National Park.

Q. What three types of magnolia trees are found in the Great Smoky Mountains National Park?

A. Umbrella magnolia (*Magnolia tripetala*), cucumber tree (*Magnolia acuminata*), and Fraser magnolia (*Magnolia fraseri*).

Q. For what mineral is the area around Henderson noted?

A. Tungsten.

Q. Near what town is there an S-shaped bridge, thought to be the only one of its kind?

A. Hertford (Highway 17 N Business).

Q. What type of rock from Grandfather Mountain is believed by geologists to be over a billion years old?

A. A granite-like gneiss.

Q. Highlands is the site of what scenic drive-through?

A. Bridal Veil Water Falls on U.S. Highway 64.

Q. In what Asheville museum can children sit on the floor and put together a human skeleton?

A. The Health Adventure.

Q. What Princeton area attraction features more than 600 varieties each of bearded irises and day lillies?

A. Powell Gardens.

Q. What city has received the Tree City, U.S.A. award numerous times from the National Arbor Day Foundation?

A. Charlotte.

◆

Q. Around the Great Dismal Swamp what beverage was at one time believed to give immunity to malaria?

A. Juniper tea.

◆

Q. What was the weight of a gold nugget found at the Reed mine in Cabarrus County in 1799?

A. Seventeen pounds.

◆

Q. What is the most visited museum in North Carolina?

A. Schiele Museum of Natural History and Planetarium.

◆

Q. In which North Carolina community was the first operation performed with the aid of a general anesthetic?

A. Jamestown, 1856.

◆

Q. Near what community is the nation's largest southern magnolia tree situated?

A. Carvers.

◆

Q. What are the most treacherous shallows on the North Carolina coast?

A. Diamond Shoals.

Q. How many varieties of flowering plants are found in the Great Smoky Mountains?

A. More than 1,300.

———◆———

Q. What three universities joined together in 1958 to form Research Triangle Park?

A. North Carolina State, Duke, and the University of North Carolina.

———◆———

Q. In what county is the William B. Umstead State Park situated?

A. Wake County.

———◆———

Q. What museum has a study collection of more than 700 catalogued mineral specimens?

A. The Museum of North Carolina Minerals, Spruce Pine.

———◆———

Q. Due to the extremely rugged terrain, what wilderness area requires that a permit be obtained before entering?

A. Linville Gorge Wilderness Area.

———◆———

Q. What North Carolina river is considered by geologists to be second only to the Nile in age?

A. The New River.

———◆———

Q. Maintaining the record for being the largest of its kind, what tree stands in Swannanoa, Burke County, with a trunk circumference of 6.5 feet?

A. A southern crab apple tree.

Q. Rare and valuable pigeon-blood rubies are found only in Mogock valley in Burma and in what location in North Carolina?

A. The Cowee valley.

———◆———

Q. What type of tree growing in Enka is recorded as the largest of its kind in the nation?

A. A weeping willow (ninety-seven feet in height, with a trunk circumference of twenty-four feet).

———◆———

Q. What municipality proclaims itself the highest incorporated community east of the Rocky Mountains?

A. Beech Mountain, elevation 5,505 feet.

———◆———

Q. The Nags Head woods have the only ponds in North Carolina where all genera of what type of aquatic plant grow?

A. Duckweed.

———◆———

Q. Where is the world's largest lithium-producing plant?

A. Bessemer City.

———◆———

Q. As a business venture, Mrs. Carl Sandburg raised what type of animal on their two-hundred-forty-acre farm at Flat Rock?

A. Nubian and Tobbenburg goats.

———◆———

Q. What material accidentally added to an open tobacco drying fire in 1852 created the first bright leaf tobacco?

A. Charcoal logs.

Q. Where is the oldest scuppernong muscadine vine found in America?

A. On private property, east of Manteo.

———————◆———————

Q. In what Guilford County town was there an attempt to establish a silkworm industry in 1839?

A. Jamestown.

———————◆———————

Q. The high-in-caffeine leaves of what evergreen are dried and brewed into tea?

A. Yaupon.

———————◆———————

Q. For what is Judaculla rock, situated near East LaPorte, noted?

A. Indian petroglyphs.

———————◆———————

Q. The Dan Nicholas Park and Nature Center is near which town?

A. Salisbury.

———————◆———————

Q. Cone Mills, Charlotte, is the world's largest manufacturer of what type of cloth?

A. Corduroy.

———————◆———————

Q. What were the six main crops grown by the original Cherokee Indians of North Carolina?

A. Corn, beans, squash, sunflowers, pumpkins, and gourds.

Q. How many varieties of salamanders have been recorded in the Great Smokies?

A. Twenty-six, more than found in any other place in the world.

———◆———

Q. Clay from what county was used by monks to fashion bricks for the building of the Belmont Abbey Church?

A. Gaston.

———◆———

Q. What North Carolina town became a bird sanctuary in 1930?

A. Statesville.

———◆———

Q. Where is the nation's largest rabbit breeders' club headquartered?

A. Monroe, Union County.

———◆———

Q. North Carolina leads the nation in the production of what mineral?

A. Feldspar.

———◆———

Q. What plant, found in Pender County, has been listed as an endangered species and is now protected by law?

A. The Venus's-Flytrap (*Dionaea muscipula*).

———◆———

Q. Grandfather Mountain is in what mountain range?

A. The Blue Ridge Mountains.

Q. Minneapolis and its surrounding area are noted for deposits of what type of mineral?

A. Amphibole asbestos.

———◆———

Q. What is the state's most common softwood tree?

A. Loblolly pine.

———◆———

Q. What city carries the nickname "City of Medicine, USA"?

A. Durham.

———◆———

Q. Because of the heavy haze, what did the Cherokees call the mountains of northwest North Carolina?

A. "The land of a thousand smokes."

———◆———

Q. What product was first marketed to the nation by Glen Raven Mills, Charlotte?

A. Pantyhose.

———◆———

Q. Where is the annual Henderson County Gem and Mineral Spectacular Show held?

A. Hendersonville.

———◆———

Q. Seven thousand species of shells from around the world may be seen in what community?

A. Ocracoke, the Alta Van Landingham Collection.

Q. What insect poses the greatest threat to the great fir and spruce trees of the Appalachians?

A. The balsam woolly aphid.

—————◆—————

Q. North America's largest Fraser fir stands in what community?

A. Cashiers, Jackson County, eighty-seven feet in height, a crown spread of fifty-two feet, and a trunk circumference of nine feet.

—————◆—————

Q. Who developed the Meish grape variety in Beaufort County?

A. Albert Meish.

—————◆—————

Q. Where was the nation's first tree farm and forestry school established?

A. On the acreage of the Biltmore mansion, which was donated to the federal government.

—————◆—————

Q. What is the North Carolina state flower?

A. Flowering dogwood (*Cornus florida*).

—————◆—————

Q. How many square miles did the Great Dismal Swamp cover originally?

A. 2,200.

—————◆—————

Q. How many tobacco seeds are there to an ounce?

A. More than 300,000.

SCIENCE & NATURE

Q. What two type of vultures may be found in North Carolina?

A. Turkey and Black vultures.

———◆———

Q. Robbins is noted for the mining of what mineral?

A. Pyrophyllite.

———◆———

Q. Where is the Lotus Blossom Festival, which features some 2,000 types of water lilies and lotus, held each year?

A. Franklin.

———◆———

Q. Who brought grass seed to Currituck County in 1720 and developed it into the timothy fodder grass?

A. Timothy Hanson.

———◆———

Q. What mountain range in North Carolina is believed by some geologists to be the oldest in North America and among the oldest in the world?

A. The Uwharrie Mountains.

———◆———

Q. Where did the first golden berry holly tree originate?

A. Lexington, officially registered as Morgan Gold.

———◆———

Q. Windsor is the home of what type of tree that has been found to be the biggest in North Carolina, according to the American Forestry Association?

A. A bald cypress, 138 feet in height, with a circumference of thirty-eight feet.

Q. What North Carolina museum features the Southeast's largest collection of North American mammals?

A. The Schiele Museum of Natural History and Planetarium.

———◆———

Q. Dropping 411 feet, what falls near Brevard is one of the highest in the eastern United States?

A. Whitewater Falls.

———◆———

Q. At what Kure Beach attraction is there a "touch tank" where visitors can handle some forms of marine life?

A. North Carolina Aquarium.

———◆———

Q. What is the second-ranking crop in North Carolina?

A. Corn.

———◆———

Q. An abundance of what type of bird can be seen and heard at Crowder's Mountain State Park?

A. Warblers, twenty species.

———◆———

Q. What is the name of the small wild horses that roamed Ocracoke Island and Cape Hatteras?

A. Wild Banker ponies.

———◆———

Q. What is the smallest state forest?

A. Tuttle State Forest, only 160 acres.

Q. What was the date of Wilbur and Orville Wright's first flight in a powered craft?

A. December 17, 1903.

———◆———

Q. Which is the largest of the Carolina Bay lakes?

A. Lake Waccamaw.

———◆———

Q. How old is North Carolina's most famous tree, the Hall of Fame Cypress, which stands on private property in New Bern?

A. Over 1,000 years.

———◆———

Q. Near what community will you find 200 acres of commercially grown tulips?

A. Terra Ceia near Pantego.

———◆———

Q. What is the primary material from which the Wright Brothers National Memorial is constructed?

A. Mount Airy granite.

———◆———

Q. The more than 300 privately owned campgrounds across the state offer how many campsites?

A. More than 15,000.

———◆———

Q. What state park features a 600-foot-high granite geological formation with a circumference of three miles at the base?

A. Stone Mountain State Park.

Q. What are the two most common trees in North Carolina?

A. Oak and pine.

———◆———

Q. What county is the leading producer of flue-cured to-bacco?

A. Pitt.

———◆———

Q. The Roanoke River empties into what body of water?

A. The Albemarle Sound.

———◆———

Q. What is the outstanding attraction at Pilot Mountain State Park?

A. A quartzite formation 1,500 feet in height.

———◆———

Q. Where was the first emerald mine in the United States?

A. Stony Point.

———◆———

Q. What flowering tree, now found in the wilds of the western half of the state, was introduced to North Carolina by George Vanderbilt?

A. The paulownia or empress tree.

———◆———

Q. The settlement of Diamond City on Shackleford Banks became famous in the nineteenth century for the cleaning, salting, packing, and shipping of what type fish?

A. Salted mullet.

Q. What North Carolina coastal park was designated in 1958 as the first National Seashore?

A. Cape Hatteras National Seashore.

Q. What county is known for its anthracite coal?

A. Moore.

Q. Who was the scientist and mathematician who was among the first group of colonists on Roanoke Island?

A. Thomas Harriot.

Q. How many new jobs were created in North Carolina by small businesses between 1983 and 1987?

A. More than 400,000.

Q. Which 3,800-acre North Carolina forest is named after the author of the poem "Trees"?

A. The Joyce Kilmer Memorial Forest.

Q. What is the North Carolina state bird?

A. Cardinal.

Q. Who was the first licensed female pharmacist in the state?

A. Emily Kyser of Rocky Mount (mother of bandleader Kay Kyser).

Q. What lake is formed by the TVA dam on the Little Tennessee River?

A. Fontana Lake.

———◆———

Q. Chimney Rock is in which county?

A. Rutherford.

———◆———

Q. Numerically, where do peanuts rank as one of North Carolina's chief products?

A. Fourth.

———◆———

Q. What two songbirds are common to North Carolina?

A. The mockingbird and the Carolina wren.

———◆———

Q. What bird did the Cherokee Indians of North Carolina consider their "great sacred bird"?

A. The eagle.

———◆———

Q. What is the most plentiful fish in North Carolina's coastal water?

A. The spot.

———◆———

Q. The three North Carolina Marine Resources Centers are found at what locations?

A. Fort Fisher, Bogue Banks, and Roanoke Island.

Q. What beautifully manicured gardens, adjacent to the site of the Lost Colony, serve as a memorial to the early settlers?

A. Elizabethan Gardens.

———◆———

Q. Where was the Milton variety of high-yield barley developed?

A. North Carolina State University.

———◆———

Q. Kaolin clay is supplied to the entire state from which three counties?

A. Avery, Mitchell, and Cleveland.

———◆———

Q. What rare sandstone is found in the Sauratown Mountains?

A. Itacolumite.

———◆———

Q. North Carolina ranks as the leading manufacturer of what building material?

A. Bricks.

———◆———

Q. What community hosts the nation's oldest gourd festival?

A. Cary, Wake County.

———◆———

Q. What is the major industry of Edenton, in Chowan County?

A. Peanuts.

Q. What three types of poisonous snakes are indigenous to North Carolina?

A. Cottonmouth, copperhead, and rattlesnake.

———◆———

Q. In what creek were large gold nuggets found, which created North Carolina's gold rush?

A. Little Meadow Creek.

———◆———

Q. Researchers at what university developed a genetically superior pine tree that has increased lumber production?

A. North Carolina State.

———◆———

Q. What was the time duration of the Wright Brothers' first powered flight?

A. Twelve seconds.

———◆———

Q. What Franklinton attraction features a large petting zoo?

A. Arkland.

———◆———

Q. What environmental program established in 1983 encourages citizen groups to become active participants in protecting and caring for local rivers, creeks, and streams?

A. "Stream Watch."

———◆———

Q. For what type of water are the Vade Mecum Springs known?

A. Alkaline water.

Q. What is the world's rarest gem, found on just a few acres in Alexander County?

A. Hiddenite.

———◆———

Q. What mountain blossoms in mid-June with more than 600 acres of rhododendron?

A. Roan Mountain.

———◆———

Q. At what facility in Latta Plantation Park near Charlotte do injured birds of prey find refuge?

A. The Carolina Raptor Center.

———◆———

Q. At its closing in 1938, the Cranberry Mine in Avery County had yielded how many tons of magnesite ore?

A. 2,000,000.

———◆———

Q. What event in Rockingham County offers the opportunity to taste daisies, cattails, peppergrass, and other familiar plants normally referred to as weeds?

A. The North Carolina Wild Foods Weekend.

———◆———

Q. What company, which moved to Matthews in 1963, now has a facility covering more than 220,000 square feet?

A. Rexham Industrial.

———◆———

Q. What University of North Carolina building was a celestial navigation training facility for NASA astronauts from 1959 to 1975?

A. Morehead Planetarium.

SCIENCE & NATURE

Q. To what type of patients did the famous 1871 "glass-house" Davis Hotel of Kittrell cater?

A. Tuberculosis patients.

———◆———

Q. Which North Carolinian from Ingleside experimented with the development of the linotype machine but never received a patent on his device?

A. Fenton Foster.

———◆———

Q. The building stone of many of the turn-of-the-century brownstone mansions of New York and Philadelphia came from what area in North Carolina?

A. Lee County.

———◆———

Q. What is the only large river in the state with both its headwaters and mouth in the same county?

A. New River.

———◆———

Q. What is the largest recorded gold nugget taken from the Reed Mine in Cabarrus County?

A. Twenty-eight pounds.

———◆———

Q. What river flows through Hickory Nut Gorge in Rutherford County?

A. The Broad River.

———◆———

Q. What type of deposits have been mined extensively near Maysville?

A. Marl deposits.

Q. What slender, grayish-stemmed, rootless plant may be seen hanging from trees in swampy areas of the state?

A. Spanish moss.

———◆———

Q. Which is the most often observed variety of woodpecker in the state?

A. The common flicker.

———◆———

Q. What tree standing in Asheville is the largest of its type in North America?

A. A two-winged silverbell 65.5 feet in height, with a crown spread of thirty-four feet.

———◆———

Q. In what county do both the Great Dover Swamp and the Whiteoak Swamp lie?

A. Jones.

———◆———

Q. The Tobacco Museum is in what town?

A. Kenly.

———◆———

Q. Cape Lookout National Seashore is well-known for what two activities loved by naturalists?

A. Primitive camping and shelling.

———◆———

Q. The Honey Bee Festival is held in what town?

A. Kernersville.